Interactive Applications Using Matplotlib

Don't just see your data, experience it!

Benjamin V. Root

BIRMINGHAM - MUMBAI

Interactive Applications Using Matplotlib

First published: March 2015

Production reference: 1170315

Published by Packt Publishing Ltd.
Livery Place
35 Livery Street
Birmingham B3 2PB, UK.

ISBN 978-1-78398-884-6

www.packtpub.com

Credits

Author

Benjamin V. Root

Reviewers

Kamran Husain

Nathan Jarus

Jens Hedegaard Nielsen

Sergi Pons Freixes

Acquisition Editors

Richard Gall

Owen Roberts

Content Development Editor

Shubhangi Dhamgaye

Technical Editors

Tanvi Bhatt

Nanda Padmanabhan

Copy Editors

Roshni Banerjee

Gladson Monteiro

Project Coordinator

Harshal Ved

Proofreaders

Maria Gould

Lesley Harrison

Bernadette Watkins

Indexer

Monica Ajmera Mehta

Production Coordinator

Conidon Miranda

Cover Work

Conidon Miranda

About the Author

Benjamin V. Root has been a member of the Matplotlib development team since 2010. His main areas of development have been the documentation and the mplot3d toolkit, but now he focuses on code reviews and debugging. Ben is also an active member of mailing lists, using his expertise to help newcomers understand Matplotlib. He is a meteorology graduate student, working part-time on his PhD dissertation. He works full-time for Atmospheric and Environmental Research, Inc. as a scientific programmer.

I would like to acknowledge the entire Matplotlib development team for their insightful responses to my questions while I was writing this book. In particular, I would like to thank Michael Droettboom, Eric Firing, Thomas Caswell, Phil Elson, and Ryan May. Thanks also go to the members of the matplotlib users' list without whom I would have never learned this tool in the first place and for whom I wrote this book.

This book would not have been possible without the love and support of my wife, Margaret. She put up with far more than she should have, and for that, I am in her debt.

Last, but not least, I must acknowledge John Hunter, the creator of Matplotlib and the man who included me into the development team. Working with him and the rest of the team allowed me to mature as a programmer and scientist, and directly resulted in me attaining my current employment, thus starting my career.

About the Reviewers

Nathan Jarus is a computer science PhD candidate at Missouri S&T. He regularly uses Matplotlib to visualize and experiment with results. Prior to his graduate studies, he spent several years developing data visualization tools for research professors. Beyond visualization, he studies complex system modeling and control.

Jens Hedegaard Nielsen is a research software developer at University College London, where he works on a number of different programming projects in relation to research across the university. He is an active Matplotlib developer. He has a PhD in experimental laser physics from Aarhus University, Denmark.

Sergi Pons Freixes is a telecommunications engineer and a PhD candidate with experience on optical sensors and data analysis. For almost 10 years, he has been working in international environments, performing both hands-on development and research.

During his master's degree in telecommunications engineering, he engaged in part-time research in the Department of Signal Theory and Communications at the Polytechnic University of Catalonia (UPC), with the design and development of a low-cost hyperspectral in-situ sensor. This experience stimulated him to start a PhD at the same department. He obtained a grant from the Spanish National Research Council (CSIC) and performed his predoctoral training at the Marine Technology Unit in Barcelona, graduating for a master of advanced studies and leading and supervising the master thesis of other university students, while continuing his research on low-cost solutions oriented to increase the observational capabilities for marine/oceanographic biological information systems.

In 2011, he gained a fellowship from the Spanish Ministry of Economy and Competitiveness to expand his experience in international scientific organisms, moving to the European Space Agency office in Italy and working on assessing the viability of remote sensing coral monitoring. During his stay, he gained a contractor position as performance simulation engineer for the Sentinel 3 satellite project at the European Space Agency facilities in the Netherlands, being responsible for the simulators and processors operation and maintenance.

In January 2015, he moved to San Diego, California, where he is currently finishing his PhD while he pursues new opportunities.

www.PacktPub.com

Support files, eBooks, discount offers, and more

For support files and downloads related to your book, please visit www.PacktPub.com.

Did you know that Packt offers eBook versions of every book published, with PDF and ePub files available? You can upgrade to the eBook version at www.PacktPub.com and as a print book customer, you are entitled to a discount on the eBook copy. Get in touch with us at service@packtpub.com for more details.

At www.PacktPub.com, you can also read a collection of free technical articles, sign up for a range of free newsletters and receive exclusive discounts and offers on Packt books and eBooks.

https://www2.packtpub.com/books/subscription/packtlib

Do you need instant solutions to your IT questions? PacktLib is Packt's online digital book library. Here, you can search, access, and read Packt's entire library of books.

Why subscribe?

- Fully searchable across every book published by Packt
- Copy and paste, print, and bookmark content
- On demand and accessible via a web browser

Free access for Packt account holders

If you have an account with Packt at www.PacktPub.com, you can use this to access PacktLib today and view 9 entirely free books. Simply use your login credentials for immediate access.

Table of Contents

Preface

Why Matplotlib? Why Python, for that matter? I picked up Python for scientific development because I needed a full-fledged programming language that made sense. Too often, I felt hemmed in by the traditional tools in the meteorology field. I needed a language that respected my time as a developer and didn't fight me every step of the way. "Don't you find Python constricting?" asked a colleague who was fond of bad puns. "No, quite the opposite," I replied, the joke going right over my head.

Matplotlib is the same in this respect. Switching from traditional graphing tools of the meteorology field to Matplotlib was a breath of fresh air. Not only were useful programs being written using the Matplotlib library, but it was also easy to write my own. Furthermore, I could write out modules and easily use them in both the hardcopy generating scripts for my publications and for my data exploration interactive applications. Most importantly, the Matplotlib library let me do what I needed it to do.

I have been an active developer for Matplotlib since 2010 and I am *still* discovering Matplotlib. It isn't that the library is insanely huge and unwieldy—it isn't. Instead, Matplotlib appeals to all levels of expertise and interests. One can simply care enough only to get a single plot displayed in three line of code and never think of the library again. Or, one could assume control over every single minute plotting detail, ensuring that everything is displayed "just right." And even when one does this and thinks they have seen every single nook and cranny of the library, they will discover some other feature that they have never seen before.

Matplotlib is 12 years old now. New plotting projects have cropped up—some supplementing Matplotlib's design, while others trying to replace Matplotlib entirely. However, there has been no slacking of interest in Matplotlib, not from the users and definitely not from the developers. The new projects are interesting, and as with all things open source, we try to learn from these projects. But I keep coming back to this project. Its design, developers, and community of users are some of the best and most devoted in the open source world.

The book you are reading right now is actually not the book I originally wanted to write. The interactive aspect of Matplotlib is not my area of expertise. After some nudging from fellow developers and users, I relented. I proceeded to rewrite the only interactive application I had ever finished and published. Working through the chapters, I tried to find better ways of doing the things I did originally, pointing out major pitfalls and easy mistakes as I encountered them. It was a significant learning experience for me, which was wholly unexpected.

I now invite you to discover Matplotlib for yourself. Whether it is the first time or not, it certainly won't be the last.

What this book covers

Chapter 1, *Introducing Interactive Plotting*, covers basic figure-axes-artist hierarchy and other Matplotlib essentials such as displaying the plot. It also introduces you to the interactive Matplotlib figure.

Chapter 2, *Using Events and Callbacks*, provides Matplotlib's events and a callback system to bring your figures to life. It also explains how you can extend it with custom events, making the application truly interactive.

Chapter 3, *Animations*, deals with ArtistAnimation, FuncAnimation, and timers to make animations of all types. It also deals with animations that can be saved as movies.

Chapter 4, *Widgets*, covers built-in widgets such as buttons, checkboxes, selectors, lassos, and sliders, which are all explained and demonstrated. Here, you'll also learn about other useful third-party widgets and tools.

Chapter 5, *Embedding Matplotlib*, teaches you how to add GUI elements to an existing Matplotlib application. Here you'll also see how to add your interactive Matplotlib figure to an existing GUI application. Identical examples are presented using GTK, Tkinter, wxWidgets, and Qt.

What you need for this book

At the absolute least, you will need the following Python packages installed on your system: NumPy, SciPy, Basemap, and (of course) Matplotlib. To work on the instructions presented in *Chapter 5, Embedding Matplotlib*, you will want to have at least one of the following GUI toolkits installed: GTK, Tkinter (should come with Python), wxWidgets, or Qt (version 4 is preferred; version 5 is supported only recently for Matplotlib version 1.4). You will also need the corresponding Python bindings for the GUI toolkits (some come with them by default).

Who this book is for

If you are a Python programmer who wants to do more than just see your data, this is the book for you. It will explain the SciPy stack (that is, NumPy and Matplotlib) and provide pointers to install them. Experience with GUI toolkits, such as wxPython, Qt, or GTK+, is also not required, so this book can be an excellent complement to other GUI programming resources. To understand the examples and explanations, you need to know basic object-oriented programming terms and concepts.

Conventions

In this book, you will find a number of text styles that distinguish between different kinds of information. Here are some examples of these styles and an explanation of their meaning.

Code words in text, database table names, folder names, filenames, file extensions, pathnames, dummy URLs, user input, and Twitter handles are shown as follows: "We can include other contexts through the use of the `include` directive."

A block of code is set as follows:

```
import matplotlib.pyplot as plt
from matplotlib.collections import LineCollection
from tutorial import track_loader
tracks = track_loader('polygons.shp')
# Filter out non-tracks (unassociated polygons given trackID of -9)
tracks = {tid: t for tid, t in tracks.items() if tid != -9}
```

When we wish to draw your attention to a particular part of a code block, the relevant lines or items are set in bold:

```python
polys = [p for p in cells.polygons]
for p in polys:
    p.set_visible(True)
    p.set_alpha(0.0)

def update(frame, polys):
    for i, p in enumerate(polys):
        alpha = 0.0 if i > frame else 1.0 / ((frame - i + 1)**2)
        p.set_alpha(alpha)

ax.set_xlabel("Longitude")
ax.set_ylabel("Latitude")
strmanim = FuncAnimation(fig, update, frameCnt,
                         fargs=(polys,))
plt.show()
```

Any command-line input or output is written as follows:

```
$ pip install matplotlib
```

New terms and **important words** are shown in bold. Words that you see on the screen, for example, in menus or dialog boxes, appear in the text like this: "Now click on the **Selection** radio button and you will find that you can select a polygon again."

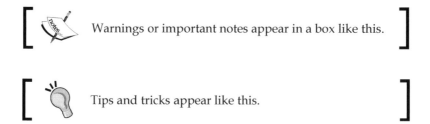

Warnings or important notes appear in a box like this.

Tips and tricks appear like this.

Reader feedback

Feedback from our readers is always welcome. Let us know what you think about this book—what you liked or disliked. Reader feedback is important for us as it helps us develop titles that you will really get the most out of.

To send us general feedback, simply e-mail `feedback@packtpub.com`, and mention the book's title in the subject of your message.

If there is a topic that you have expertise in and you are interested in either writing or contributing to a book, see our author guide at `www.packtpub.com/authors`.

Customer support

Now that you are the proud owner of a Packt book, we have a number of things to help you to get the most from your purchase.

Downloading the example code

You can download the example code files from your account at `http://www.packtpub.com` for all the Packt Publishing books you have purchased. If you purchased this book elsewhere, you can visit `http://www.packtpub.com/support` and register to have the files e-mailed directly to you.

Errata

Although we have taken every care to ensure the accuracy of our content, mistakes do happen. If you find a mistake in one of our books—maybe a mistake in the text or the code—we would be grateful if you could report this to us. By doing so, you can save other readers from frustration and help us improve subsequent versions of this book. If you find any errata, please report them by visiting `http://www.packtpub.com/submit-errata`, selecting your book, clicking on the **Errata Submission Form** link, and entering the details of your errata. Once your errata are verified, your submission will be accepted and the errata will be uploaded to our website or added to any list of existing errata under the Errata section of that title.

To view the previously submitted errata, go to `https://www.packtpub.com/books/content/support` and enter the name of the book in the search field. The required information will appear under the **Errata** section.

Piracy

Piracy of copyrighted material on the Internet is an ongoing problem across all media. At Packt, we take the protection of our copyright and licenses very seriously. If you come across any illegal copies of our works in any form on the Internet, please provide us with the location address or website name immediately so that we can pursue a remedy.

Please contact us at copyright@packtpub.com with a link to the suspected pirated material.

We appreciate your help in protecting our authors and our ability to bring you valuable content.

Questions

If you have a problem with any aspect of this book, you can contact us at questions@packtpub.com, and we will do our best to address the problem.

1
Introducing Interactive Plotting

A picture is worth a thousand words

The goal of any interactive application is to provide as much information as possible while minimizing complexity. If it can't provide the information the users need, then it is useless to them. However, if the application is too complex, then the information's signal gets lost in the noise of the complexity. A graphical presentation often strikes the right balance.

The Matplotlib library can help you present your data as graphs in your application. Anybody can make a simple interactive application without knowing anything about draw buffers, event loops, or even what a GUI toolkit is. And yet, the Matplotlib library will cede as much control as desired to allow even the most savvy GUI developer to create a masterful application from scratch. Like much of the Python language, Matplotlib's philosophy is to give the developer full control, but without being stupidly unhelpful and tedious.

Installing Matplotlib

There are many ways to install Matplotlib on your system. While the library used to have a reputation for being difficult to install on non-Linux systems, it has come a long way since then, along with the rest of the Python ecosystem. Refer to the following command:

```
$ pip install matplotlib
```

Most likely, the preceding command would work just fine from the command line. Python Wheels (the next-generation Python package format that has replaced "eggs") for Matplotlib are now available from PyPi for Windows and Mac OS X systems. This method would also work for Linux users; however, it might be more favorable to install it via the system's built-in package manager.

While the core Matplotlib library can be installed with few dependencies, it is a part of a much larger scientific computing ecosystem known as SciPy. Displaying your data is often the easiest part of your application. Processing it is much more difficult, and the SciPy ecosystem most likely has the packages you need to do that. For basic numerical processing and N-dimensional data arrays, there is NumPy. For more advanced but general data processing tools, there is the SciPy package (the name was so catchy, it ended up being used to refer to many different things in the community). For more domain-specific needs, there are "Sci-Kits" such as `scikit-learn` for artificial intelligence, `scikit-image` for image processing, and `statsmodels` for statistical modeling. Another very useful library for data processing is `pandas`.

This was just a short summary of the packages available in the SciPy ecosystem. Manually managing all of their installations, updates, and dependencies would be difficult for many who just simply want to use the tools. Luckily, there are several distributions of the SciPy Stack available that can keep the menagerie under control. The following are Python distributions that include the SciPy Stack along with many other popular Python packages or make the packages easily available through package management software:

- Anaconda from Continuum Analytics
- Canopy from Enthought
- SciPy Superpack
- Python(x, y) (Windows only)
- WinPython (Windows only)
- Pyzo (Python 3 only)
- Algorete Loopy from Dartmouth College

For this book, we will assume at least Python 2.7 or 3.2. The requisite packages are `numpy`, `matplotlib`, `basemap`, and `scipy`. Just about any version of these packages released in the past 3 years should work for most examples in this book (exceptions are noted in this book). The version 0.14.0 of SciPy (released in May 2014) *cannot* be used in this book due to a (now fixed) regression in its NetCDF reader. *Chapter 5, Embedding Matplotlib* will have special notes with regards to GUI toolkit packages.

Show() your work

With Matplotlib installed, you are now ready to make your first simple plot. Matplotlib has multiple layers. `Pylab` is the topmost layer, often used for quick one-off plotting from within a live Python session. Start up your favorite Python interpreter and type the following:

```
>>> from pylab import *
>>> plot([1, 2, 3, 2, 1])
```

Nothing happened! This is because Matplotlib, by default, will not display anything until you explicitly tell it to do so. The Matplotlib library is often used for automated image generation from within Python scripts, with no need for any interactivity. Also, most users would not be done with their plotting yet and would find it distracting to have a plot come up automatically. When you are ready to see your plot, use the following command:

```
>>> show()
```

Interactive navigation

A figure window should now appear, and the Python interpreter is not available for any additional commands. By default, showing a figure will block the execution of your scripts and interpreter. However, this does not mean that the figure is not interactive. As you mouse over the plot, you will see the plot coordinates in the lower right-hand corner. The figure window will also have a toolbar:

From left to right, the following are the tools:

- **Home, Back, and Forward**: These are similar to that of a web browser. These buttons help you navigate through the previous views of your plot. The "Home" button will take you back to the first view when the figure was opened. "Back" will take you to the previous view, while "Forward" will return you to the previous views.

- **Pan (and zoom)**: This button has two modes: pan and zoom. Press the left mouse button and hold it to pan the figure. If you press *x* or *y* while panning, the motion will be constrained to just the *x* or *y* axis, respectively. Press the right mouse button to zoom. The plot will be zoomed in or out proportionate to the right/left and up/down movements. Use the *X, Y,* or *Ctrl* key to constrain the zoom to the x axis or the y axis or preserve the aspect ratio, respectively.

- **Zoom-to-rectangle**: Press the left mouse button and drag the cursor to a new location and release. The axes view limits will be zoomed to the rectangle you just drew. Zoom out using your right mouse button, placing the current view into the region defined by the rectangle you just drew.

- **Subplot configuration**: This button brings up a tool to modify plot spacing.

- **Save**: This button brings up a dialog that allows you to save the current figure.

The figure window would also be responsive to the keyboard. The default keymap is fairly extensive (and will be covered fully later), but some of the basic hot keys are the *Home* key for resetting the plot view, the left and right keys for back and forward actions, *p* for pan/zoom mode, *o* for zoom-to-rectangle mode, and *Ctrl + s* to trigger a file save. When you are done viewing your figure, close the window as you would close any other application window, or use *Ctrl + w*.

Interactive plotting

When we did the previous example, no plots appeared until show() was called. Furthermore, no new commands could be entered into the Python interpreter until all the figures were closed. As you will soon learn, once a figure is closed, the plot it contains is lost, which means that you would have to repeat all the commands again in order to show() it again, perhaps with some modification or additional plot. Matplotlib ships with its **interactive plotting mode** off by default.

There are a couple of ways to turn the interactive plotting mode on. The main way is by calling the ion() function (for Interactive ON). Interactive plotting mode can be turned on at any time and turned off with ioff(). Once this mode is turned on, the next plotting command will automatically trigger an implicit show() command. Furthermore, you can continue typing commands into the Python interpreter. You can modify the current figure, create new figures, and close existing ones at any time, all from the current Python session.

Scripted plotting

Python is known for more than just its interactive interpreters; it is also a fully fledged programming language that allows its users to easily create programs. Having a script to display plots from daily reports can greatly improve your productivity. Alternatively, you perhaps need a tool that can produce some simple plots of the data from whatever mystery data file you have come across on the network share. Here is a simple example of how to use Matplotlib's pyplot API and the argparse Python standard library tool to create a simple CSV plotting script called plotfile.py.

Code: chp1/plotfile.py

```python
#!/usr/bin/env python

from argparse import ArgumentParser
import matplotlib.pyplot as plt

if __name__ == '__main__':
    parser = ArgumentParser(description="Plot a CSV file")
    parser.add_argument("datafile", help="The CSV File")
    # Require at least one column name
    parser.add_argument("columns", nargs='+',
                        help="Names of columns to plot")
    parser.add_argument("--save", help="Save the plot as...")
    parser.add_argument("--no-show", action="store_true",
                        help="Don't show the plot")
    args = parser.parse_args()

    plt.plotfile(args.datafile, args.columns)
    if args.save:
        plt.savefig(args.save)
    if not args.no_show:
        plt.show()
```

Note the two optional command-line arguments: --save and --no-show. With the --save option, the user can have the plot automatically saved (the graphics format is determined automatically from the filename extension). Also, the user can choose not to display the plot, which when coupled with the --save option might be desirable if the user is trying to plot several CSV files.

When calling this script to show a plot, the execution of the script will stop at the call to plt.show(). If the interactive plotting mode was on, then the execution of the script would continue past show(), terminating the script, thus automatically closing out any figures before the user has had a chance to view them. This is why the interactive plotting mode is turned off by default in Matplotlib.

Also note that the call to `plt.savefig()` is *before* the call to `plt.show()`. As mentioned before, when the figure window is closed, the plot is lost. You cannot save a plot after it has been closed.

Getting help

We have covered how to install Matplotlib and went over how to make very simple plots from a Python session or a Python script. Most likely, this went very smoothly for you. The rest of this book will focus on how to use Matplotlib to make an interactive application, rather than the many ways to display data. You may be very curious and want to learn more about the many kinds of plots this library has to offer, or maybe you want to learn how to make new kinds of plots.

Help comes in many forms. The Matplotlib website (`http://matplotlib.org`) is the primary online resource for Matplotlib. It contains examples, FAQs, API documentation, and, most importantly, the gallery.

Gallery

Many users of Matplotlib are often faced with the question, "I want to make a plot that has this data along with that data in the same figure, but it needs to look like this other plot I have seen." Text-based searches on graphing concepts are difficult, especially if you are unfamiliar with the terminology. The gallery showcases the variety of ways in which one can make plots, all using the Matplotlib library. Browse through the gallery, click on any figure that has pieces of what you want in your plot, and see the code that generated it. Soon enough, you will be like a chef, mixing and matching components to produce that perfect graph.

Mailing lists and forums

When you are just simply stuck and cannot figure out how to get something to work or just need some hints on how to get started, you will find much of the community at the Matplotlib-users mailing list. This mailing list is an excellent resource of information with many friendly members who just love to help out newcomers. Be persistent! While many questions do get answered fairly quickly, some will fall through the cracks. Try rephrasing your question or with a plot showing your attempts so far. The people at Matplotlib-users love plots, so an image that shows what is wrong often gets the quickest response. A newer community resource is StackOverflow, which has many very knowledgeable users who are able to answer difficult questions.

From front to backend

So far, we have shown you bits and pieces of two of Matplotlib's topmost abstraction layers: pylab and pyplot. The layer below them is the object-oriented layer (the OO layer). To develop any type of application, you will want to use this layer. Mixing the pylab/pyplot layers with the OO layer will lead to very confusing behaviors when dealing with multiple plots and figures.

Below the OO layer is the backend interface. Everything above this interface level in Matplotlib is completely platform-agnostic. It will work the same regardless of whether it is in an interactive GUI or comes from a driver script running on a headless server. The backend interface abstracts away all those considerations so that you can focus on what is most important: writing code to visualize your data.

There are several backend implementations that are shipped with Matplotlib. These backends are responsible for taking the figures represented by the OO layer and interpreting it for whichever "display device" they implement. The backends are chosen automatically but can be explicitly set, if needed (see *Chapter 5, Embedding Matplotlib*).

Interactive versus non-interactive

There are two main classes of backends: ones that provide interactive figures and ones that don't. Interactive backends are ones that support a particular GUI, such as Tcl/Tkinter, GTK, Qt, Cocoa/Mac OS X, wxWidgets, and Cairo. With the exception of the Cocoa/Mac OS X backend, all interactive backends can be used on Windows, Linux, and Mac OS X. Therefore, when you make an interactive Matplotlib application that you wish to distribute to users of any of those platforms, unless you are embedding Matplotlib (again, see *Chapter 5, Embedding Matplotlib*), you will not have to concern yourself with writing a single line of code for any of these toolkits—it has already been done for you!

Non-interactive backends are used to produce image files. There are backends to produce Postscript/EPS, Adobe PDF, and **Scalable Vector Graphics (SVG)** as well as rasterized image files such as PNG, BMP, and JPEGs.

Anti-grain geometry

The open secret behind the high quality of Matplotlib's rasterized images is its use of the Anti-Grain Geometry (AGG) library (http://agg.sourceforge.net/antigrain.com/index.html). The quality of the graphics generated from AGG is far superior than most other toolkits available. Therefore, not only is AGG used to produce rasterized image files, but it is also utilized in most of the interactive backends as well. Matplotlib maintains and ships with its own fork of the library in order to ensure you have consistent, high quality image products across all platforms and toolkits. What you see on your screen in your interactive figure window will be the same as the PNG file that is produced when you call savefig().

Selecting your backend

When you install Matplotlib, a default backend is chosen for you based upon your OS and the available GUI toolkits. For example, on Mac OS X systems, your installation of the library will most likely set the default interactive backend to MacOSX or CocoaAgg for older Macs. Meanwhile, Windows users will most likely have a default of TkAgg or Qt5Agg. In most situations, the choice of interactive backends will not matter. However, in certain situations, it may be necessary to force a particular backend to be used. For example, on a headless server without an active graphics session, you would most likely need to force the use of the non-interactive Agg backend:

```
import matplotlib
matplotlib.use("Agg")
```

When done prior to any plotting commands, this will avoid loading any GUI toolkits, thereby bypassing problems that occur when a GUI fails on a headless server. Any call to show() effectively becomes a no-op (and the execution of the script is not blocked). Another purpose of setting your backend is for scenarios when you want to embed your plot in a native GUI application. Therefore, you will need to explicitly state which GUI toolkit you are using (see *Chapter 5, Embedding Matplotlib*). Finally, some users simply like the look and feel of some GUI toolkits better than others. They may wish to change the default backend via the backend parameter in the matplotlibrc configuration file. Most likely, your rc file can be found in the .matplotlib directory or the .config/matplotlib directory under your home folder. If you can't find it, then use the following set of commands:

```
>>> import matplotlib
>>> matplotlib.matplotlib_fname()
u'/home/ben/.config/matplotlib/matplotlibrc'
```

Here is an example of the relevant section in my `matplotlibrc` file:

```
#### CONFIGURATION BEGINS HERE

# the default backend; one of GTK GTKAgg GTKCairo GTK3Agg
# GTK3Cairo CocoaAgg MacOSX QtAgg Qt4Agg TkAgg WX WXAgg Agg Cairo
# PS PDF SVG
# You can also deploy your own backend outside of matplotlib by
# referring to the module name (which must be in the PYTHONPATH)
# as 'module://my_backend'
#backend      : GTKAgg
#backend      : QT4Agg
backend       : TkAgg
# If you are using the Qt4Agg backend, you can choose here
# to use the PyQt4 bindings or the newer PySide bindings to
# the underlying Qt4 toolkit.
#backend.qt4 : PyQt4        # PyQt4 | PySide
```

This is the global configuration file that is used if one isn't found in the current working directory when Matplotlib is imported. The settings contained in this configuration serves as default values for many parts of Matplotlib. In particular, we see that the choice of backends can be easily set without having to use a single line of code.

The Matplotlib figure-artist hierarchy

Everything that can be drawn in Matplotlib is called an **artist**. Any artist can have child artists that are also drawable. This forms the basis of a hierarchy of artist objects that Matplotlib sends to a backend for rendering. At the root of this artist tree is the **figure**.

In the examples so far, we have not explicitly created any figures. The `pylab` and `pyplot` interfaces will create the figures for us. However, when creating advanced interactive applications, it is highly recommended that you explicitly create your figures. You will especially want to do this if you have multiple figures being displayed at the same time. This is the entry into the OO layer of Matplotlib:

```
fig = plt.figure()
```

Canvassing the figure

The figure is, quite literally, your canvas. Its primary component is the `FigureCanvas` instance upon which all drawing occurs. Unless you are embedding your Matplotlib figures into a GUI application, it is very unlikely that you will need to interact with this object directly. Instead, as plotting commands are issued, artist objects are added to the canvas automatically.

While any artist can be added directly to the figure, usually only **Axes** objects are added. A figure can have many axes objects, typically called **subplots**. Much like the figure object, our examples so far have not explicitly created any axes objects to use. This is because the `pylab` and `pyplot` interfaces will also automatically create and manage axes objects for a figure if needed. For the same reason as for figures, you will want to explicitly create these objects when building your interactive applications. If an axes or a figure is not provided, then the `pyplot` layer will have to make assumptions about which axes or figure you mean to apply a plotting command to. While this might be fine for simple situations, these assumptions get hairy very quickly in non-trivial applications. Luckily, it is easy to create both your figure and its axes using a single command:

```
fig, axes = plt.subplots(2, 1)  # 2x1 grid of subplots
```

These objects are highly advanced complex units that most developers will utilize for their plotting needs. Once placed on the figure canvas, the axes object will provide the ticks, axis labels, axes title(s), and the plotting area. An axes is an artist that manages all of its scale and coordinate transformations (for example, log scaling and polar coordinates), automated tick labeling, and automated axis limits. In addition to these responsibilities, an axes object provides a wide assortment of plotting functions. A sampling of plotting functions is as follows:

Function	Description
bar	Make a bar plot
barbs	Plot a two-dimensional field of barbs
boxplot	Make a box and whisker plot
cohere	Plot the coherence between x and y
contour	Plot contours
errorbar	Plot an errorbar graph
hexbin	Make a hexagonal binning plot
hist	Plot a histogram
imshow	Display an image on the axes
pcolor	Create a pseudocolor plot of a two-dimensional array
pcolormesh	Plot a quadrilateral mesh

Function	Description
pie	Plot a pie chart
plot	Plot lines and/or markers
quiver	Plot a two-dimensional field of arrows
sankey	Create a Sankey flow diagram
scatter	Make a scatter plot of x versus y
stem	Create a stem plot
streamplot	Draw streamlines of a vector flow

Throughout the rest of this book, we will build a single interactive application piece by piece, demonstrating concepts and features that are available through Matplotlib. This application will be a storm track editing application. Given a series of radar images, the user can circle each storm cell they see in the radar image and link those storm cells across time. The application will need the ability to save and load track data and provide the user with mechanisms to edit the data. Along the way, we will learn about Matplotlib's structure, its artists, the callback system, doing animations, and finally, embedding this application within a larger GUI application.

So, to begin, we first need to be able to view a radar image. There are many ways to load data into a Python program but one particular favorite among meteorologists is the **Network Common Data Form (NetCDF)** file. The SciPy package has built-in support for NetCDF version 3, so we will be using an hour's worth of radar reflectivity data prepared using this format from a NEXRAD site near Oklahoma City, OK on the evening of May 10, 2010, which produced numerous tornadoes and severe storms.

The NetCDF binary file is particularly nice to work with because it can hold multiple data variables in a single file, with each variable having an arbitrary number of dimensions. Furthermore, metadata can be attached to each variable and to the dataset itself, allowing you to self-document data files. This particular data file has three variables, namely Reflectivity, lat, and lon to record the radar reflectivity values and the latitude and longitude coordinates of each pixel in the reflectivity data. The reflectivity data is three-dimensional, with the first dimension as time and the other two dimensions as latitude and longitude. The following code example shows how easy it is to load this data and display the first image frame using SciPy and Matplotlib.

Code: chp1/simple_radar_viewer.py

```
import matplotlib.pyplot as plt
from scipy.io import netcdf_file

ncf = netcdf_file('KTLX_20100510_22Z.nc')
data = ncf.variables['Reflectivity']
lats = ncf.variables['lat']
lons = ncf.variables['lon']
i = 0

cmap = plt.get_cmap('gist_ncar')
cmap.set_under('lightgrey')

fig, ax = plt.subplots(1, 1)
im = ax.imshow(data[i], origin='lower',
               extent=(lons[0], lons[-1], lats[0], lats[-1]),
               vmin=0.1, vmax=80, cmap='gist_ncar')
cb = fig.colorbar(im)

cb.set_label('Reflectivity (dBZ)')
ax.set_xlabel('Longitude')
ax.set_ylabel('Latitude')
plt.show()
```

Running this script should result in a figure window that will display the first frame of our storms that we will become very familiar with over the next few chapters. The plot has a colorbar and the axes ticks label the latitudes and longitudes of our data. What is probably most important in this example is the imshow() call. Being an image, traditionally, the origin of the image data is shown in the upper-left corner and Matplotlib follows this tradition by default. However, this particular dataset was saved with its origin in the lower-left corner, so we need to state this with the origin parameter. The extent parameter is a tuple describing the data extent of the image. By default, it is assumed to be at (0, 0) and (N - 1, M - 1) for an MxN shaped image. The vmin and vmax parameters are a good way to ensure consistency of your colormap regardless of your input data. If these two parameters are not supplied, then imshow() will use the minimum and maximum of the input data to determine the colormap. This would be undesirable as we move towards displaying arbitrary frames of radar data. Finally, one can explicitly specify the colormap to use for the image. The gist_ncar colormap is very similar to the official NEXRAD colormap for radar data, so we will use it here:

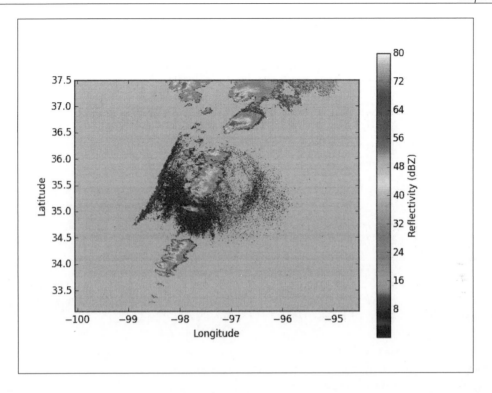

 The gist_ncar colormap, along with some other colormaps packaged with Matplotlib such as the default jet colormap, are actually terrible for visualization. See the *Choosing Colormaps* page of the Matplotlib website for an explanation of why, and guidance on how to choose a better colormap.

The menagerie of artists

Whenever a plotting function is called, the input data and parameters are processed to produce new artists to represent the data. These artists are either **primitives** or collections thereof. They are called primitives because they represent basic drawing components such as lines, images, polygons, and text. It is with these primitives that your data can be represented as bar charts, line plots, errorbars, or any other kinds of plots.

Primitives

There are four drawing primitives in Matplotlib: Line2D, AxesImage, Patch, and Text. It is through these primitive artists that all other artist objects are derived from, and they comprise everything that can be drawn in a figure.

A Line2D object uses a list of coordinates to draw line segments in between. Typically, the individual line segments are straight, and curves can be approximated with many vertices; however, curves can be specified to draw arcs, circles, or any other Bezier-approximated curves.

An AxesImage class will take two-dimensional data and coordinates and display an image of that data with a colormap applied to it. There are actually other kinds of basic image artists available besides AxesImage, but they are typically for very special uses. AxesImage objects can be very tricky to deal with, so it is often best to use the imshow() plotting method to create and return these objects.

A Patch object is an arbitrary two-dimensional object that has a single color for its "face." A polygon object is a specific instance of the slightly more general patch. These objects have a "path" (much like a Line2D object) that specifies segments that would enclose a face with a single color. The path is known as an "edge," and can have its own color as well. Besides the Polygons that one sees for bar plots and pie charts, Patch objects are also used to create arrows, legend boxes, and the markers used in scatter plots and elsewhere.

Finally, the Text object takes a Python string, a point coordinate, and various font parameters to form the text that annotates plots. Matplotlib primarily uses TrueType fonts. It will search for fonts available on your system as well as ship with a few FreeType2 fonts, and it uses Bitstream Vera by default. Additionally, a Text object can defer to LaTeX to render its text, if desired.

While specific artist classes will have their own set of properties that make sense for the particular art object they represent, there are several common properties that can be set. The following table is a listing of some of these properties.

Property	Meaning
alpha	0 represents transparent and 1 represents opaque
color	Color name or other color specification
visible	boolean to flag whether to draw the artist or not
zorder	value of the draw order in the layering engine

Let's extend the radar image example by loading up already saved polygons of storm cells in the tutorial.py file.

Code: chp1/simple_storm_cell_viewer.py

```python
import matplotlib.pyplot as plt
from scipy.io import netcdf_file
from matplotlib.patches import Polygon
from tutorial import polygon_loader

ncf = netcdf_file('KTLX_20100510_22Z.nc')
data = ncf.variables['Reflectivity']
lats = ncf.variables['lat']
lons = ncf.variables['lon']
i = 0

cmap = plt.get_cmap('gist_ncar')
cmap.set_under('lightgrey')

fig, ax = plt.subplots(1, 1)
im = ax.imshow(data[i], origin='lower',
               extent=(lons[0], lons[-1], lats[0], lats[-1]),
               vmin=0.1, vmax=80, cmap='gist_ncar')
cb = fig.colorbar(im)

polygons = polygon_loader('polygons.shp')
for poly in polygons[i]:
    p = Polygon(poly, lw=3, fc='k', ec='w', alpha=0.45)
    ax.add_artist(p)
cb.set_label("Reflectivity (dBZ)")
ax.set_xlabel("Longitude")
ax.set_ylabel("Latitude")
plt.show()
```

The polygon data returned from `polygon_loader()` is a dictionary of lists keyed by a frame index. The list contains Nx2 numpy arrays of vertex coordinates in longitude and latitude. The vertices form the outline of a storm cell. The Polygon constructor, like all other artist objects, takes many optional keyword arguments. First, `lw` is short for `linewidth`, (referring to the outline of the polygon), which we specify to be three points wide. Next is `fc`, which is short for `facecolor`, and is set to black (`'k'`). This is the color of the filled-in region of the polygon. Then `edgecolor` (`ec`) is set to white (`'w'`) to help the polygons stand out against a dark background. Finally, we set the `alpha` argument to be slightly less than half to make the polygon fairly transparent so that one can still see the reflectivity data beneath the polygons.

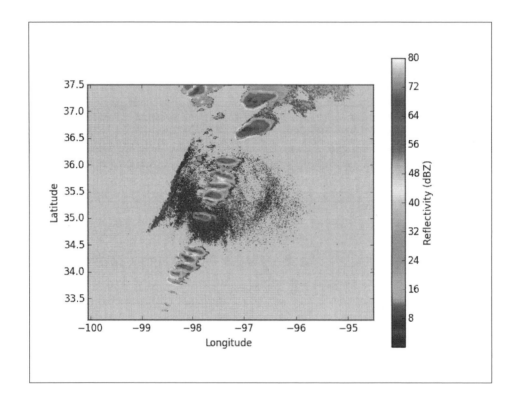

Note a particular difference between how we plotted the image using `imshow()` and how we plotted the polygons using polygon artists. For polygons, we called a constructor and then explicitly called `ax.add_artist()` to add each polygon instance as a child of the axes. Meanwhile, `imshow()` is a plotting function that will do all of the hard work in validating the inputs, building the `AxesImage` instance, making all necessary modifications to the axes instance (such as setting the limits and aspect ratio), and most importantly, adding the artist object to the axes. Finally, all plotting functions in Matplotlib return artists or a list of artist objects that it creates. In most cases, you will not need to save this return value in a variable because there is nothing else to do with them. In this case, we only needed the returned `AxesImage` so that we could pass it to the `fig.colorbar()` method. This is so that it would know what to base the colorbar upon.

The plotting functions in Matplotlib exist to provide convenience and simplicity to what can often be very tricky to get right by yourself. They are not magic! They use the same OO interface that is accessible to application developers. Therefore, anyone can write their own plotting functions to make complicated plots easier to perform.

Collections

Any artist that has child artists (such as a figure or an axes) is called a **container**. A special kind of container in Matplotlib is called a **Collection**. A collection usually contains a list of primitives of the same kind that should all be treated similarly. For example, a CircleCollection would have a list of Circle objects, all with the same color, size, and edge width. Individual values for artists in the collection can also be set. A collection makes management of many artists easier. This becomes especially important when considering the number of artist objects that may be needed for scatter plots, bar charts, or any other kind of plot or diagram.

Some collections are not just simply a list of primitives, but are artists in their own right. These special kinds of collections take advantage of various optimizations that can be assumed when rendering similar or identical things. `RegularPolyCollection`, for example, just needs to know the points of a single polygon relative to its center (such as a star or box) and then just needs a list of all the center coordinates, avoiding the need to store all the vertices of every polygon in its collection in memory.

In the following example, we will display storm tracks as `LineCollection`. Note that instead of using `ax.add_artist()` (which would work), we will use `ax.add_collection()` instead. This has the added benefit of performing special handling on the object to determine its bounding box so that the axes object can incorporate the limits of this collection with any other plotted objects to automatically set its own limits which we trigger with the `ax.autoscale(True)` call.

Code: `chp1/linecoll_track_viewer.py`

```python
import matplotlib.pyplot as plt
from matplotlib.collections import LineCollection
from tutorial import track_loader

tracks = track_loader('polygons.shp')
# Filter out non-tracks (unassociated polygons given trackID of -9)
tracks = {tid: t for tid, t in tracks.items() if tid != -9}

fig, ax = plt.subplots(1, 1)
lc = LineCollection(tracks.values(), color='b')
ax.add_collection(lc)
ax.autoscale(True)
ax.set_xlabel("Longitude")
ax.set_ylabel("Latitude")
plt.show()
```

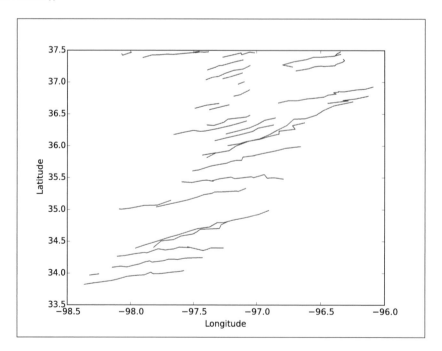

Much easier than the radar images, Matplotlib took care of all the limit setting automatically. Such features are extremely useful for writing generic applications that do not wish to concern themselves with such details. We will come back to the handling of `LineCollections` later in the book as we develop this application.

Summary

In this chapter, we introduced you to the foundational concepts of Matplotlib. Using `show()`, you showed your first plot with only three lines of Python. With this plot up on your screen, you learned some of the basic interactive features built into Matplotlib, such as panning, zooming, and the myriad of key bindings that are available. Then we discussed the difference between interactive and non-interactive plotting modes and the difference between scripted and interactive plotting. You now know where to go online for more information, examples, and forum discussions of Matplotlib when it comes time for you to work on your next Matplotlib project. Next, we discussed the architectural concepts of Matplotlib: backends, figures, axes, and artists.

Then we started our construction project for this book, an interactive storm cell tracking application. We saw how to plot a radar image using a pre-existing plotting function, as well as how to display polygons and lines as artists and collections. While creating these objects, we had a glimpse of how to customize the properties of these objects for our display needs, learning some of the property and styling names. We also learned some of the steps one needs to consider when creating their own plotting functions, such as autoscaling.

In the next chapter, we will learn how to extend the basic interactivity of Matplotlib, adding our own features and controls in order to make a truly interactive application.

2
Using Events and Callbacks

Wait time is the worst

I can hardly sit

No one has the time

Someone is always late

- The Strokes, Call Me Back (2011)

The callback system in Matplotlib is central to its interactivity. Unless you are working with the interactive plotting mode on, execution of the script stops when `plt.show()` is called. Without the ability to execute any additional code, the only way to program interactivity is to register actions to be taken upon some event such as a button click, mouse cursor motion, or key press. Matplotlib's callback system has a base set of events and many callbacks that we have already discussed, such as the default keymap discussed in the previous chapter and the ability to pan a plot. Furthermore, it is possible to add new kinds of events, giving the developer full access to Matplotlib's cross-platform callback system.

Making the connection

The callback system is figure-oriented. Any GUI action that can trigger a callback can only happen to whichever figure window is currently in focus. There are no global actions that can trigger callbacks across multiple figures. The callback function will get an **Event** object that contains pertinent information about the fired event. In the following example, we will hook up two events to a figure: a keyboard button press and a mouse button press. There are two callback functions, each printing out some of the available pieces of information for their respective events:

Code: `chp2/basic_mpl_connect.py`

```
from __future__ import print_function
import matplotlib.pyplot as plt

def process_key(event):
    print("Key:", event.key)
def process_button(event):
    print("Button:", event.x, event.y, event.xdata, event.ydata,
            event.button)

fig, ax = plt.subplots(1, 1)
fig.canvas.mpl_connect('key_press_event', process_key)
fig.canvas.mpl_connect('button_press_event', process_button)
plt.show()
```

Now, go ahead and click around in the figure window and press some keys on your keyboard. You will see all sorts of output in your terminal. We have called the `mpl_connect()` method of the figure's canvas twice—once for each action we wanted to register with each kind of event in that figure. If you had multiple figures, then the connections have to be made for each figure that you want to have for that action. The `mpl_connect()` method takes two arguments: the name of the event and the callable object (such as a function).

Event Name	Type	Typical use
`'resize_event'`	ResizeEvent	Trigger redraws due to change in figure size
`'draw_event'`	DrawEvent	Background updating or cursor clearing after a plot is refreshed
`'key_press_event'`	KeyEvent	Keymap
`'key_release_event'`	KeyEvent	Exit a temporary mode entered by holding a key down

Event Name	Type	Typical use
`'button_press_event'`	`MouseEvent`	Clicking on the mouse and the start of some button-hold action such as panning
`'button_release_event'`	`MouseEvent`	Exit a temporary mode by holding a button down such as panning
`'scroll_event'`	`MouseEvent`	This event is available, but not used in the default interaction system
`'motion_notify_event'`	`MouseEvent`	Update cursor location display in the figure, and calculate motion estimate for live panning and zooming of a plot
`'pick_event'`	`PickEvent`	Artist selection
`'idle_event'`	`IdleEvent`	This event is available, but not used in the default interaction system
`'figure_enter_event'`	`Event`	This event is available, but not used in the default interaction system
`'figure_leave_event'`	`LocationEvent`	This event is available, but not used in the default interaction system
`'axes_enter_event'`	`LocationEvent`	This event is available, but not used in the default interaction system
`'axes_leave_event'`	`LocationEvent`	This event is available, but not used in the default interaction system
`'close_event'`	`CloseEvent`	Terminates active animations

Probably the two most common events are `key_press_event` and `button_press_event` that we just discussed in the previous example. Different types of events have different information available for the callback function to use:

- `Event`: This event type provides the name string, the canvas instance, and the originating backend-specific `guiEvent`, if applicable. The name is useful if a callback function is to be attached to multiple events and needs to differentiate between them, and it can also be used for logging purposes. The `canvas` object is useful when the callback needs to trigger a canvas draw. The `guiEvent` object is usually only used for figure embedding. This is the base event type.

- `ResizeEvent`: This event type provides the height and width of the new figure in pixels.

- `DrawEvent`: This event type provides the `renderer` instance, which is important for any further draws that are needed by the callback.

- `LocationEvent`: This event type provides two types of location data. First, it provides the x and y values as pixels from the canvas' left and bottom edges, respectively. Second, it provides the `xdata` and `ydata` values as the data coordinates for the cursor when it passes over a plot axes. Furthermore, it also provides the `inaxes` attribute pointing to the `Axes` object that mouse is currently over (or `None` if not over any plot axes). This event type serves as the basis for `MouseEvent` and `KeyEvent`.

- `MouseEvent`: This event provides data on the button that triggered the event in addition to the location data of the mouse cursor. It can have numerical values of 1, 2, or 3, indicating which of the three traditional mouse buttons are active (1 is typically the left button, while 3 is the middle button or both the left and right buttons at the same time). If a key was pressed while this mouse event was triggered, the `key` attribute will indicate that key (see `KeyEvent` for more detail). The "up" and "down" `button` values indicate that the event is a scrolling event. The amount of scrolling is given by the `step` attribute, with positive values for up and negative values for down.

- `KeyEvent`: This event type provides data on the key that was either pressed or released in addition to the location data of the mouse cursor (if available). Note that modifier keys *Ctrl*, *Alt*, and **super** are prepended to the pressed key with a plus sign (for example, *"control+m"* and *"alt+control+g"*). Special keys are usually spelled out; such as *"home"* or *"up"*.

- `PickEvent`: This event type provides the `mouseevent` attribute, which is the original `MouseEvent` object that triggered the pick. This event is fired off whenever a mouse click is sufficiently close to an artist object, which is called "picking". You can use this object to obtain location data, mouse button used and any keys that were pressed at the time. The `artist` attribute contains the `Artist` object for which the mouse "picked." If multiple artists are close enough to a particular mouse click, then this is triggered for each Artist separately. Furthermore, when picking a `Collection` artist, the event object will also have an `ind` attribute that contains a list of indexes of the members of that collection that were "picked."

- `IdleEvent`: This event type contains no extra information than the base `Event` type. It serves only to flag when the GUI's event loop is idle so that developers can perform deferrable actions when the resources are available to do so. Prior to the creation of the animation module in Matplotlib and the cross-platform timer class (discussed in the next chapter), this event type was used as an ad-hoc timer for basic animations.

- `CloseEvent`: This contains no extra information than the base `Event` type, just like `IdleEvent`. This event type indicates that a figure is in the process of being closed. This is particularly useful for interactive applications to perform any sort of clean-up and bookkeeping actions whenever a figure window gets closed for whatever reason. A particular nuance about this event is that it is typically triggered at the beginning of the closing procedure. Because of that, the canvas object and everything on it *should* still be valid. However, in some cases (particularly when it is the exiting of the Python interpreter that is triggering the window closing), some objects may already be garbage-collected. Therefore, defensive programming for the `close_event` callback functions is important, particularly to guard against the `AttributeError` exceptions. Also, there is no way for a callback attached to this event to prevent the figure from closing (so you can't use this event to ask the user "Are you sure?").

The big event

What is the purpose of interactive plotting? Why is it important for Matplotlib to provide this feature? It is important because you want to *interact* with your data. What you plot in the figure is a visual representation of your data, and giving it interactivity brings that data an extra step closer to the real world by providing your users the means to interact with that data in a more physically intuitive manner. It is all about *data exploration*.

So far, for our project, we have only developed the means to display our storm and radar data. While we could simply use these viewers and then manually edit the associated shapefile, it would not be practical. We should be able to provide users the means to interrogate their data. To do this, we will use `pick_event` to add the ability to select and deselect some tracks. As a simple example, we will make a track thicker when it is selected and make it thinner when it is deselected (or simply, selected again). Let's build upon the track viewer example discussed in the previous chapter:

Code: chp2/linecoll_selector.py

```
import matplotlib.pyplot as plt
from matplotlib.collections import LineCollection
from tutorial import track_loader

def onpick(event):
    if not isinstance(event.artist, LineCollection):
        return

    lws = event.artist.get_linewidths()
```

```
        for i in event.ind:
            lws[i] = 4 if lws[i] != 4 else 1
        event.artist.set_linewidths(lws)
        fig.canvas.draw_idle()

    tracks = track_loader('polygons.shp')
    # Filter out non-tracks (unassociated polygons given trackID of -9)
    tracks = {tid: t for tid, t in tracks.items() if tid != -9}

    fig, ax = plt.subplots(1, 1)
    lc = LineCollection(tracks.values(), color='b', lw=[1]*len(tracks),
                        picker=True)
    ax.add_collection(lc)
    ax.autoscale(True)

    fig.canvas.mpl_connect('pick_event', onpick)
    ax.set_xlabel("Longitude")
    ax.set_ylabel("Latitude")
    plt.show()
```

Run this example and start clicking on some of the lines. Notice that if you click a point within a couple pixels of two or more tracks, they will all change thickness. Let's study this example for a moment, as there are several key pieces in place here to make this example work. First, for the LineCollection constructor, we are supplying a list of ones to the lw argument (for line widths), even though it defaults to a line width of one. This is because we will need to modify the line widths of individual elements; therefore, we will need to operate on a list rather than the default tuple of length one. Second, we need to set the picker argument to True in order for the collection to even be considered for picking.

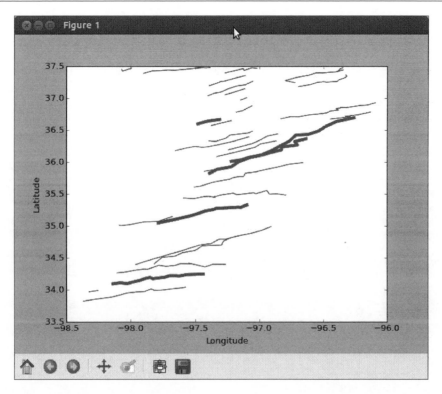

Next, notice that we protected the callback function with a type check. As our applications get more and more complex, it becomes a good idea to ensure that your particular callback is operating only on objects that you expected to operate on. In this case, it was done via a type check, but in other cases, some other sort of validation may be needed. Finally, notice that we triggered a `draw_idle()` call after updating the collection. Matplotlib will not automatically perform any draw calls for us after picking, so we need to trigger it ourselves when appropriate. Typically, we could use `draw_idle()`, but `draw()` is also valid. The difference between the two is that each `draw()` call is guaranteed to happen, while `draw_idle()` merely guarantees that a draw will occur soon, with possibly multiple queued idle draws being consolidated.

For this example, we modified line widths as our callback action, but that is not the only thing which can be modified. We could have changed line colors, transparency, or even line styles such as making the line be dashed or dotted—just about anything is possible within a callback function.

While being able to make a track appear thick or thin at our whim might give us a passing sensation of omnipotence, nothing useful is happening yet. First, the program doesn't know which track was selected, only that some tracks are thicker than others, which completely violates the separation of data and style. Second, we only want to work on a single track at a time, so we need to keep at most one track selected. Let's extend the example a bit more to include those requirements, as well as the ability to delete the selected track by pressing the *d* key.

Code: `chp2/linecoll_deleter.py`

```python
import matplotlib.pyplot as plt
from matplotlib.collections import LineCollection
from tutorial import track_loader

selected = None
def onpick(event):
    global selected
    if event.artist is not lc:
        return
    lws = lc.get_linewidths()

    ind = event.ind[0]
    if ind != selected:
        # "Select" this track
        # But first, we need to de-select the previous selection
        if selected is not None:
            lws[selected] = 1
        lws[ind] = 4
        selected = ind
    else:
        # "Deselect" this track
        lws[ind] = 1
        selected = None
    lc.set_linewidths(lws)
    fig.canvas.draw_idle()

def keypress(event):
    global selected
    if event.key == 'd' and selected is not None:
        segs = lc.get_segments()
        segs.pop(selected)
        selected = None
        lc.set_segments(segs)
        # Also need to reset the linewidths list
```

```
            lc.set_linewidths([1] * len(segs))
            fig.canvas.draw_idle()

tracks = track_loader('polygons.shp')
# Filter out non-tracks (unassociated polygons given trackID of -9)
tracks = {tid: t for tid, t in tracks.items() if tid != -9}

fig, ax = plt.subplots(1, 1)
lc = LineCollection(tracks.values(), color='b', lw=[1]*len(tracks),
                    picker=True)
ax.add_collection(lc)
ax.autoscale(True)

fig.canvas.mpl_connect('pick_event', onpick)
fig.canvas.mpl_connect('key_press_event', keypress)
ax.set_xlabel("Longitude")
ax.set_ylabel("Latitude")
plt.show()
```

We now have two callbacks, each for a different kind of event and each working off some common piece of data – the line collection object and the selected index. Add the ability to save the tracks to a file and we will have a rudimentary storm track editor!

Let's take a break from the track part of our project for a bit and work on the radar and polygon viewer some more. The viewer we developed in the first chapter was only able to show a single radar frame, which is completely useless for studying storm cells throughout their lifecycle. Let's extend that example to allow the user to move backwards and forwards in time with the left and right arrow buttons.

As you may have noticed in the previous example, we violated an age-old programming rule of avoiding global variables. Our application became complex enough that a state (the line collection and the selection index) had to be held outside the callback functions. Global variables are a very tempting way of handling this requirement, but it isn't the only way. In the following example, we will need to hold a similar state, the radar data, the polygon data, and the currently displayed frame index. We will now see a much cleaner alternative to using global variables by creating a ControlSys class that will hold the state, provide various callback functions and even connect them for you.

This example modifies the radar viewer example given in the first chapter to add a `ControlSys` class that will provide the functionality of stepping through a radar animation using the left and right arrows. It is important to save the instantiated class into a variable to prevent the object from being garbage-collected prior to calling `show()`:

Code: `chp2/stormcell_anim.py`

```python
import matplotlib.pyplot as plt
from scipy.io import netcdf_file
from matplotlib.collections import PolyCollection
from tutorial import polygon_loader

class ControlSys:
    def __init__(self, fig, im, data, polycolls):
        self.fig = fig
        self.im = im
        self.data = data
        self.polygons = polycolls
        self.i = 0
        self.fig.canvas.mpl_connect('key_press_event', self.keypress)

    def keypress(self, event):
        previ = self.i
        if event.key == 'left' and self.i > 0:
            self.i -= 1
        elif event.key=='right' and self.i < (self.data.shape[0] - 1):
            self.i += 1
        if previ != self.i:
            self.polygons[previ].set_visible(False)
            self.polygons[self.i].set_visible(True)
            self.im.set_data(self.data[self.i])
            self.fig.canvas.draw_idle()

ncf = netcdf_file('KTLX_20100510_22Z.nc')
data = ncf.variables['Reflectivity']
lats = ncf.variables['lat']
lons = ncf.variables['lon']
i = 0

cmap = plt.get_cmap('gist_ncar')
```

```
cmap.set_under('lightgrey')

fig, ax = plt.subplots(1, 1)
im = ax.imshow(data[i], origin='lower',
               extent=(lons[0], lons[-1], lats[0], lats[-1]),
               vmin=0.1, vmax=80, cmap='gist_ncar')
cb = fig.colorbar(im)

polygons = polygon_loader('polygons.shp')
polycolls = []
for frame in sorted(polygons):
    pc = PolyCollection(polygons[frame], linewidths=3, facecolors='k',
                        edgecolors='w', alpha=0.6, visible=not frame)
    ax.add_collection(pc)
    polycolls.append(pc)
ax.autoscale(True)

ctrl_sys = ControlSys(fig, im, data, polycolls)

cb.set_label("Reflectivity (dBZ)")
ax.set_xlabel("Longitude")
ax.set_ylabel("Latitude")
plt.show()
```

Another difference between this example and the original noninteractive viewer is that this time, all of the polygons across time are plotted as a `PolyCollection` for each frame, but the `visible` attribute was only set to `True` for one frame at a time. This makes it easy to selectively display the polygons based on the current frame because all that is needed to be done is to change the visibility attribute.

Breaking up is the easiest thing to do

Try the previous radar example again. This time, go forward a few frames and then zoom in with the zoom tool. Now go back a frame.

Go ahead, I'll wait.

Surprised? Remember that Matplotlib has its own built-in keymap. In the default keymap, the left arrow means to go back to a previous view. When we zoomed in and then pressed the left arrow key, not only did we go back a frame via our callback, but we also went back to the original view prior to zooming via Matplotlib's default keymap. The default keymap is a very important and useful feature for providing basic interactivity for most users. However, when developing your own application using Matplotlib, you might want to disable Matplotlib's keymap entirely. The following example shows how to do that while demonstrating the next important feature of the callback system: disconnecting a callback. In this example, you can now press any non-system key or combination of keys without ever triggering a built-in Matplotlib key press action. Go ahead and try some combinations as well:

Code: chp2/disable_mpl_keymap.py

```
from __future__ import print_function
import matplotlib.pyplot as plt

def process_key(event):
    print(event.key)

fig, ax = plt.subplots(1, 1)
fig.canvas.mpl_connect('key_press_event', process_key)
fig.canvas.mpl_disconnect(fig.canvas.manager.key_press_handler_id)
plt.show()
```

Now add that the `mpl_disconnect()` line to our radar viewer example and try the steps again. It stepped back a frame like you expected and it did not zoom out. You are now free to build up your own keymap without worry of colliding with Matplotlib's built-in keymap.

The `mpl_disconnect()` line takes a callback ID, and it will remove that callback from the event it was connected to. Every time you connect a callback function to an event using `mpl_connect()`, an ID is returned. If that particular function is already connected to that particular event, then the existing ID is returned again. That ID is returned so that the developer can choose to disconnect the event early for whatever reason. A callback function can be connected to multiple events, and each connection gets its own unique ID. So, disconnecting one of those callback connections only disconnects it from that one event.

So why would someone want to be able to disconnect a callback early? The most common use case is to set up a clean-up action upon a key or button release. Let's consider the storm cell viewer again. Even though the polygons are transparent, a user comes back with a feature request to be able to "hide" the polygons so that he can have an unobstructed view of the radar image under them. Let's implement this feature by hiding the current frame's polygons only when the *H* button is held down (let's reserve *h* for help later). Here is an updated `ControlSys` class:

Source: `chp2/stormcell_anim_with_hide.py`

```
class ControlSys:
    def __init__(self, fig, im, data, polycolls):
        self.fig = fig
        self.im = im
        self.data = data
        self.polygons = polycolls
        self.i = 0
        # Deactivate the default keymap
        keypressid = fig.canvas.manager.key_press_handler_id
        fig.canvas.mpl_disconnect(keypressid)
        self._keycid = self.fig.canvas.mpl_connect('key_press_event',
                                                   self.keypress)
        self._hidecid = None

    def keypress(self, event):
        previ = self.i
        if event.key == 'left' and self.i > 0:
            self.i -= 1
        elif event.key == 'right' and self.i < (self.data.shape[0]-1):
            self.i += 1
        elif event.key == 'H':
            if self._keycid is not None:
                self.fig.canvas.mpl_disconnect(self._keycid)
                self._keycid = None
            cid = self.fig.canvas.mpl_connect('key_release_event',
                                              self.release_hide)
            self.polygons[self.i].set_visible(False)
            self.fig.canvas.draw_idle()
        if previ != self.i:
            self.polygons[previ].set_visible(False)
            self.polygons[self.i].set_visible(True)
            self.im.set_data(self.data[self.i])
```

```
                self.fig.canvas.draw_idle()

        def release_hide(self, event):
            if event.key == 'H' and self._hidecid is not None:
                self.fig.canvas.mpl_disconnect(self._hidecid)
                self._hidecid = None
                cid = self.fig.canvas.mpl_connect('key_press_event',
                                                  self.keypress)
                self.polygons[self.i].set_visible(True)
                self.fig.canvas.draw_idle()
```

When the `ControlSys` is initialized, it makes the first connection for key press events and records it as `self._keycid`. It also instantiates a `self._hidecid` with a `None` so that we can avoid any potential missing attributes in other parts of the code. Then, when the *H* key is pressed down, we disconnect the `self.keypress()` callback and connect the `self.release_hide()` callback to the key release event, recording that connection's ID in `self._hidecid`. We also then set the current frame's polygons to invisible and perform a draw to update the display.

As long as the user does not release the *H* key, the polygons will not be visible. Also, during this time, no other key presses will activate our keymap, thereby preventing the user from inadvertently changing the frame while in this mode and invalidating our state. Once the *H* key is released, the key release event is disconnected and our keymap is reconnected, along with setting the polygons' visibility to `True` and updating the display again. The polygons are now visible, and we can still step back and forth through time and use the polygon-hiding feature again. We will see more examples of this technique when we start using widgets in *Chapter 4, Widgets*.

Keymapping

We can see that our application is going to grow in complexity very soon add we continue to add features. Our current manner of keymapping is probably not going to be easily maintainable as the number of actions increase. Let's take a moment to implement something better. The most essential feature of a keymap is to tie a predefined action to an arbitrary key or key combination. This seems like the perfect job for a dictionary. Furthermore, as the keymap grows, it will become important to be able to display the keymap in a helpful manner to your users. Each key/action pair will need to come with a description that can later be displayed on demand. Also, keeping in mind that our `ControlSys` class is likely to grow in complexity soon, let's implement this keymap feature as a separate class that `ControlSys` will inherit. The code is as follows:

Source: `chp2/stormcell_anim_with_keymap.py`

```python
class KeymapControl:
    def __init__(self, fig):
        self.fig = fig
        # Deactivate the default keymap
        keypressid = fig.canvas.manager.key_press_handler_id
        fig.canvas.mpl_disconnect(keypressid)
        self._keymap = OrderedDict()
        # Activate my keymap
        self.connect()
        self._lastkey = None

    def connect_keymap(self):
        self._keycid = self.fig.canvas.mpl_connect('key_press_event',
                                                   self.keypress)

    def disconnect_keymap(self):
        if self._keycid is not None:
            self.fig.canvas.mpl_disconnect(self._keycid)
            self._keycid = None

    def add_key_action(self, key, description, action_func):
        if not callable(action_func):
            raise ValueError("Invalid action. Key '%s' Description %s"
                             " - action function is not a callable" %
                             (key, description))
        if key in self._keymap:
            raise ValueError("'%s' is already in the keymap" % key)
        self._keymap[key] = (description, action_func)

    def keypress(self, event):
        action_tuple = self._keymap.get(event.key, None)
        if action_tuple:
            self._lastkey = event.key
            # perform callback
            action_tuple[1]()

    def display_help_menu(self):
        print("Help Menu")
        print("Key         Action")
        print("========== =========================================")
        for key, (description, _) in self._keymap.items():
            print("%11s %s" % (key, description))
```

In the code snippet, we completely rewrote the `keypress()` method to check the keymap dictionary and call the stored callable if it was available for the pressed key. The `KeymapControl` constructor creates the `OrderedDict` object that is our keymap. This class also provides convenient methods for connecting and disconnecting this keymap, along with a method to build the keymap and display a help menu. The new `display_help_menu()` method will loop over the keymap dictionary and display the keys and their respective help description. It should be noted that this is why an `OrderedDict` was used as opposed to a regular dictionary object. With an ordered dictionary, we can ensure that the menu will display related help items together such as the left and right arrow keys.

Now, let's rework the `ControlSys` class. It will subclass `KeymapControl`, so we need to factor away its `keypress()` method into two new methods: `change_frame()` and `enable_hide()`, which represent the two generalized actions that `keypress()` was performing before based on which key was pressed. The `ControlSys` constructor, once it initializes the `KeymapControl` class, can then call `add_key_action()` for each key that we wish to empower with an action. The left and right arrow keys are tied to a lambda function that calls the new `change_frame()` method with a value of `-1` and `1`, respectively. The lambdas are needed because we need to supply the keymap with a callable that it can use later. The *H* key is tied to the new `enable_hide()` method. No lambdas were needed here because this method does not need to be called with any parameters. Finally, the constructor also adds a new key action, `h`, to display a useful help menu.

An interesting complication arises with this refactor though. The `release_hide()` method needs to check that the key being released is the same key that originally triggered the hide mode. Originally, this was explicitly set as a check for the *H* value. However, with a dictionary-based keymap, we can no longer make that assumption. In fact, it is theoretically possible now for multiple keys to be tied to a single action. So, we need that method to check the event key against some saved value that will be set by the `enable_hide()` method, thus ensuring that the key used for starting the hide mode is used for turning it off. However, how do we get the `enable_hide()` method to know what key triggered it? There are a number of ways to do this. One very simple approach that you may have noticed in the `KeymapControl` class is to have the `keypress()` method record a `_lastkey` attribute for every successful keymap trigger. Now, `enable_hide()` can use `_lastkey` to record the active hide key:

Source: `chp2/stormcell_anim_with_keymap.py`

```
class ControlSys(KeymapControl):
    def __init__(self, fig, im, data, polycolls):
        self.fig = fig
```

```python
        self.im = im
        self.data = data
        self.polygons = polycolls
        self.i = 0
        self._hidekey = None
        self._hidecid = None
        KeymapControl.__init__(self, fig)

        self.add_key_action('left', 'Back a frame',
                            lambda : self.change_frame(-1))
        self.add_key_action('right', 'Forward a frame',
                            lambda : self.change_frame(1))
        self.add_key_action('H', 'Hide polygons while holding',
                            self.enable_hide)
        self.add_key_action('h', 'Display this help menu',
                            self.display_help_menu)

    def change_frame(self, frame_delta):
        newi = self.i + frame_delta
        if newi >= self.data.shape[0]:
            newi = self.data.shape[0] - 1
        if newi < 0:
            newi = 0
        if newi != self.i:
            self.polygons[self.i].set_visible(False)
            self.polygons[newi].set_visible(True)
            self.im.set_data(self.data[newi])
            self.fig.canvas.draw_idle()
            self.i = newi

    def enable_hide(self):
        self.disconnect_keymap()
        self._hidekey = self._lastkey.lower()
        cid = self.fig.canvas.mpl_connect('key_release_event',
                                          self.release_hide)
        self._hidecid = cid
        self.polygons[self.i].set_visible(False)
        self.fig.canvas.draw_idle()

    def release_hide(self, event):
        key = event.key.lower()
        if key == self._hidekey and self._hidecid is not None:
```

```
self.fig.canvas.mpl_disconnect(self._hidecid)
self._hidekey = None
self._hidecid = None
self.connect_keymap()
self.polygons[self.i].set_visible(True)
self.fig.canvas.draw_idle()
```

Besides the improved scalability of this keymap design, we also gain better modularity by defining a method for each separate action. These actions could now be triggered in other ways than just through the keymap. This makes unit testing easier, which is always a plus. Also, this design makes it easier to customize the keymap. As you will see in a later section on user-defined events, we will be able to externally define the keymap in a user configuration file. A further improvement would be to have the keymapped callables return `True` or `False` to indicate that a change in the state has occurred. The `keypress()` method could then trigger a call to the `draw_idle()` method instead of having the callables do that. This would be a further separation of responsibilities for the methods so that methods like `change_frame()` could be used outside of any interactive drawing context such as automated unit tests.

Picking

We demonstrated pick events earlier, showing how to select a storm track, changing its thickness, but we haven't incorporated picking into our current design yet. Much in the same vein as the `KeymapControl` class, let's create a `PickControl` class that will keep a list of pick functions (pickers) and manage their connection to the callback system for us:

Source: `chp2/select_stormcells.py`

```
class PickControl:
    def __init__(self, fig):
        self.fig = fig
        self._pickers = []
        self._pickcids = []

    def connect_picks(self):
        for i, picker in enumerate(self._pickers):
            if self._pickcids[i] is None:
```

```
                    cid = self.fig.canvas.mpl_connect('pick_event',
                                                      picker)
                    self._pickcids[i] = cid

        def disconnect_picks(self):
            for i, cid in enumerate(self._pickcids):
                if cid is not None:
                    self.fig.canvas.mpl_disconnect(cid)
                    self._pickcids[i] = None

        def add_pick_action(self, picker):
            if not callable(picker):
                raise ValueError("Picker function is not callable")
            if  picker in self._pickers:
                raise ValueError("Picker is already in the list
            self._pickers.append(picker)
            cid = self.fig.canvas.mpl_connect('pick_event', picker)
            self._pickcids.append(cid)
```

Because we will be selecting storm cells instead of tracks, we need to modify the construction of the PolyCollections to have a list of line widths as well as setting the picker argument to True, much like we did back in the track selection example for LineCollections. Next, we need to have ControlSys inherit from both KeymapControl and PickControl, and register a new ControlSys method for picking:

Source: chp2/select_stormcells.py

```
        def select_stormcell(self, event):
            if event.artist not in self.polygons:
                return
            ind = event.ind[0]
            lws = event.artist.get_linewidths()
            if (self.i, ind) != self.selected:
                if self.selected is not None:
                    prev_i, prev_ind = self.selected
                    prev_lws = self.polygons[prev_i].get_linewidths()
                    prev_lws[prev_ind] = 1
                    self.polygons[prev_i].set_linewidths(prev_lws)

                lws[ind] = 4
```

```
        self.selected = (self.i, ind)
    else:
        lws[ind] = 1
        self.selected = None

    event.artist.set_linewidths(lws)
    self.fig.canvas.draw_idle()
```

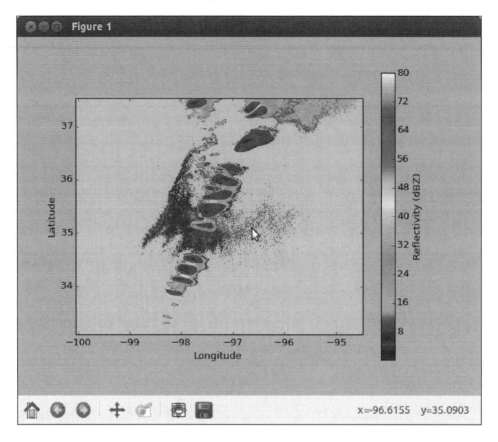

In the original track selection example, the `selected` variable was kept as a global variable, which was a bad coding practice. Now, it is safely managed as an attribute of the `ControlSys` class. Another difference between how we implemented track and storm cell selection is that the `selected` variable now holds a tuple of the frame index and the index within the polygon collection for that frame. This was necessary as it requires two dimensions to properly reference a given `Polygon` artist in our application as opposed to a single dimension for a single `Line2D` artist.

Data editing

Sometimes, it is easy to lose sight of your original goals when developing an application. We have been so focused on adding all sorts of bells and whistles to this project that we have forgotten about its most important purpose: the *editing* of storm cells and their tracks. Our application, so far, is strictly a data viewer, and a limited one at that. We are not able to interrogate the display for more information about the features we see, nor are we able to save our changes, much less even make any changes. We demonstrated a track deletion feature back in the beginning of the chapter, but that information could not be linked back to the source dataset for modification.

It is at the beginning of an application development that one must be very careful. It is very easy to conflate the display with the data, as we have already done. Conflating data and display can cause two kinds of problems. First, your data can become tied up in some obscure, inscrutable display object that may or may not respect the integrity of your original data. For example, our vertexes for the storm cell polygons are currently stored in a `PolyCollection` object. It is not out of the realm of possibility that Matplotlib could apply a path simplification algorithm to the supplied points in order to reduce the amount of drawing it needs to perform. The same applies to the tracks and the `LineCollection` object. The second problem that can happen with conflating data and display is a tunnel vision that can hinder the developer's design. The original dataset could contain extra information, such as the size of the storm cell, its intensity, and so on. So far, our viewer application has completely ignored this data because we didn't need it for the narrow-focused task of simply displaying tracks and polygons. This resulted in nearly "painting ourselves into a corner" with our application. If we had developed it further while conflating the display and the data, we would have made it costly to restructure the code to integrate the complete dataset into the application.

Now that we need to be able to round-trip our data from input to output and back to input for a new instance of the editor, we will discontinue the use of the `polygon_loader()` and `track_loader()` functions, and start using the `storm_loader()` function instead.

The NumPy primer

The `storm_loader()` and `storm_saver()` functions use a data object known as a **NumPy structured array**. NumPy arrays are generalized *n*-dimensional arrays containing values that all share the same type (called a `dtype`). This is ideal for dealing with datasets since algorithms and storage can be optimized when all the values of the array are of the same size. A NumPy array can be sliced and indexed much like a Python list. A structured array is a special kind of NumPy array that has a compound dtype (that is, multiple basic data types together as one, such as two floats and an integer). A compound dtype can have names associated with each of the component dtypes. Consider the following example:

```
points = np.array([(.0, 1), (.4, 2), (.6, 3), (.2, 1)],
                  dtype=[('y', 'f'), ('t', 'i')])
```

The preceding command creates a structured array of length four and two named parts. We can access this array in one of two ways: by record (indexing and/or slicing) and by header (dictionary access). Both `points[2:4]['y']` and `points['y'][2:4]` will produce the same result. This allows two ways of managing the data using the same object.

As part of the separation of the data and the display, we will need a way to map information between the two. This is important because we will need to maintain the integrity of our data structures as the editor is used. The following code snippet shows the modification of the creation of the `PolyCollection` objects from the raw storm data:

Source: chp2/stormcell_editor.py

```
stormcells = storm_loader('polygons.shp')
polycolls = []
stormmap = []
for frame in range(np.max(stormcells['frame_index']) + 1):
    indexes = np.where(stormcells['frame_index'] == frame)[0]
    polygons = stormcells[indexes]['poly']
    pc = PolyCollection(polygons, lw=[1]*len(polygons),
                        facecolors='k', edgecolors='w', alpha=0.6,
                        visible=(not frame), picker=True)
    ax.add_collection(pc)
    polycolls.append(pc)
    stormmap.append(indexes)
```

In addition to the `polycolls` list that we had before, we will keep a `stormmap` list containing NumPy arrays of indexes, referencing each storm cell's location in the original `stormcells` data object. Notice that NumPy arrays can be sliced in additional ways that normal Python lists cannot. In this snippet, the `stormcells` array was indexed by a NumPy array of indexes, producing a new NumPy array that is a subset of the original. Another way to index a NumPy array is to use a NumPy array of Booleans, which will also produce a subset of the original data array. That method is called Boolean indexing, and it will be demonstrated in the next code snippet.

We now need to update the ControlSys constructor to include the storm cell data object and the mapping array. We will also add two new keymapped actions: `delete_selected()` and `save_stormdata()` tied to the *d* and *w* keys, respectively (*w* is for write). The `delete_selected()` method will not only delete the polygon from the frame's `PolyCollection`, it will also have to remove it from the data object as well as update the information contained in the mapping array. As for the `save_stormdata()` method, we will have the data saved to a differently named file for now to prevent clobbering the original packaged file. We will eventually want to parameterize the filename arguments for better control:

Source: chp2/stormcell_editor1.py

```python
class ControlSys(KeymapControl, PickControl):
    def __init__(self, fig, im, data, polygons, stormdata, stormmap):
        self.fig = fig
        self.im = im
        self.data = data
        self.i = 0
        self.selected = None
        self.polygons = polygons
        self.stormdata = stormdata
        self.stormmap = stormmap
        self._hidekey = None
        self._hidecid = None
        KeymapControl.__init__(self, fig)
        PickControl.__init__(self, fig)

        self.add_key_action('left', 'Back a frame',
                            lambda : self.change_frame(-1))
        self.add_key_action('right', 'Forward a frame',
                            lambda : self.change_frame(1))
        self.add_key_action('H', 'Hide polygons while holding',
                            self.enable_hide)
        self.add_key_action('d', 'Delete the selected storm cell',
                            self.delete_selected)
```

```
            self.add_key_action('w', 'Save the storm data',
                                 self.save_stormdata)
            self.add_key_action('h', 'Display this help menu',
                                 self.display_help_menu)
            self.add_pick_action(self.select_stormcell)

    def delete_selected(self):
        if self.selected is None:
            return
        # only delete when the selection is in the current frame
        if self.i != self.selected[0]:
            return

        stormcell_index = self.stormmap[self.i][self.selected[1]]
        # Take it out of the raw stormdata object and everywhere else
        self.stormdata = np.delete(self.stormdata, stormcell_index)
        self.stormmap[self.i] = np.delete(self.stormmap[self.i],
                                          self.selected[1])
        paths = self.polygons[self.i].get_paths()
        paths.pop(self.selected[1])
        self.polygons[self.i].set_linewidths([1] * len(paths))

        # Also decrement any indexes greater than stormcell_index
        for indexes in self.stormmap:
            indexes[indexes > stormcell_index] -= 1
        self.selected = None
        self.fig.canvas.draw_idle()

    def save_stormdata(self):
        storm_saver('polygons_new.shp', self.stormdata)
```

The `delete_selected()` method takes advantage of various NumPy features to manage the data that we have. First, NumPy provides a `delete()` function for its arrays. This is useful because NumPy arrays cannot change size, so such convenience functions paper over the fact that you are receiving a copy of the original array with that particular element removed. This is done for both the raw `stormdata` and the appropriate element in the `stormmap` array. Next, the appropriate polygon is removed by "popping" its path data out of the collection. The line width data is also reset to the appropriate length. Finally, the rest of the `stormmap` data is updated. This loops over the list of NumPy arrays, decrementing any value that was greater than the index of the storm cell we just removed. This particular action is what uses Boolean indexing to find all elements in `indexes` that were greater than a particular value.

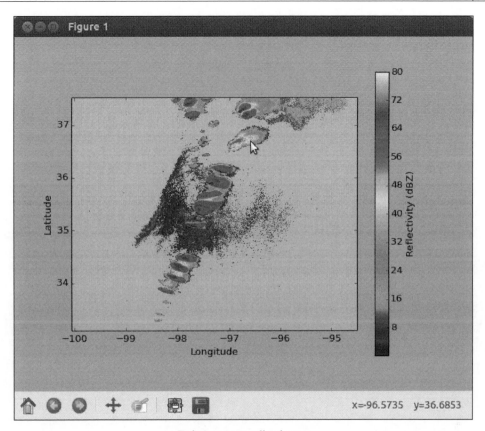

Deleting storm cell polygons

The `stormcell_editor1.py` file that we just completed is a functional editor. It can select and delete storm cells, and those changes can get saved to a file. However, it is not very extensible. The display elements are intertwined with the control elements, which only serves to make our control code more confusing. Confusing code is difficult to maintain and hard to reuse.

We are going to need to improve how the code is organized so that we can continue developing towards the interactive storm cell editor. There are two primary display items in our editor: the radar display and the storm cell polygons. This was easy enough to manage in `ControlSys`, but we still haven't added all of our display elements. It is time to spin these things off into their own classes. The radar display class is easy to make:

Source: chp2/stormcell_editor2.py

```
class RadarDisplay(object):
    def __init__(self, ax, lats, lons):
        self.im = None
```

```
        cmap = plt.get_cmap('gist_ncar')
        cmap.set_under('lightgrey')
        self.initialize_display(ax, lats, lons)

    def initialize_display(self, ax, lats, lons):
        if self.im is not None:
            self.im.remove()
        fake_data = np.zeros((lats.shape[0], lons.shape[0]))
        self.im = ax.imshow(fake_data, origin='lower',
            extent=(lons[0], lons[-1], lats[0], lats[-1]),
            vmin=0.1, vmax=80, cmap='gist_ncar')

    def update_display(self, data):
        self.im.set_data(data)
```

Some of you may be scratching your heads, "Why didn't we initialize the display with the radar data?" The answer is that this design enforces the separation of the data and the display. This class merely provides the needed functionality to show a particularly sized radar display, complete with a preset color map and positioning. Next, we will create the Stormcells class. This is a bit more involved, but you will find a lot of familiar code:

Source: chp2/stormcell_editor2.py

```
class Stormcells(object):
    def __init__(self, ax, stormdata):
        self.polygons = []
        self.create_polygons(ax, stormdata)

    @staticmethod
    def create_stormmap(stormdata):
        frame_cnt = np.max(stormdata['frame_index']) + 1
        stormmap = [np.where(stormdata['frame_index'] == frame)[0]
                    for frame in range(frame_cnt)]
        return stormmap

    def remove_polygons(self):
        for strm in self.polygons:
            strm.remove()
        self.polygons = []

    def create_polygons(self, ax, stormdata):
        # Clear any previously existing polygons
```

```
            self.remove_polygons()

            for indexes in self.create_stormmap(stormcells):
                polygons = stormdata[indexes]['poly']
                pc = PolyCollection(polygons, lw=[1]*len(polygons),
                        facecolors='k', zorder=1, edgecolors='w',
                        alpha=0.45, picker=True, visible=False)
                ax.add_collection(pc)
                self.polygons.append(pc)

    def delete_polygon(self, inds):
        frame_i, cell_i = inds
        paths = self.polygons[frame_i].get_paths()
        paths.pop(cell_i)
        lws = self.polygons[frame_i].get_linewidths()
        lws.pop(cell_i)

    def toggle_polygons(self, frame_index, visible=None):
        if visible is None:
            visible = not self.polygons[frame_index].get_visible()
        self.polygons[frame_index].set_visible(visible)

    def lolite_polygon(self, inds):
        self.hilite_polygon(inds, 1)

    def hilite_polygon(self, inds, lw=4):
        if inds is not None:
            frame_i, cell_i = inds
            lws = self.polygons[frame_i].get_linewidths()
            lws[cell_i] = lw
            self.polygons[frame_i].set_linewidths(lws)
```

Many of these methods are largely unaltered from ControlSys and the main logic. That is another advantage of the work we are doing: simplifying the main logic by encapsulating components into their own classes. The primary reason for encapsulating these items into their own classes is to facilitate any future changes that may come with regards to how we implement specific display elements.

Another important feature you can see is that while this class will construct a storm map data structure (and even use it when creating polygons), it will not store it for itself. This is again another design decision for the separation of the data and display. Undoubtedly, the storm map is needed to establish the relationship between the display object and the data, but the hard question is, "Who should own it?" By its very nature, both `ControlSys` and `Stormcells` could make credible claims to that data structure. Ultimately, the question came down to which class needed the storm map more. While the `Stormcells` class needs it when building the polygons, it is only in relation to accessing the original data structure. Meanwhile, the `ControlSys` needs it for managing interactivity, and is also in the best position for maintaining the structure during any changes to the data. Therefore, while the `Stormcells` class provides the static method for creating the storm map, it will be the `ControlSys` that will obtain that map and maintain it.

User events

We have now seen our storm cell editing application grow in complexity as we start adding even just a few features. The stormcell editor has a gamut of interactive features and can delete storm cells and save the edited stormcells. And for good measure, this application is cross-platform and can work using just about any of the major GUI toolkits that are available, all in approximately 200 lines of code. Now, before we start patting ourselves on the back, there is still a lot more to be done. The editor still does not display any storm tracks, which will be another set of artists to manage along with the storm cell polygons. The track and storm cell display will need to be maintained together as they share a common underlying data. For example, the selection of a track should also trigger a selection of a storm cell in that track, and vice versa. The deletion of a storm cell should also trigger an update of its track line.

Managing all of this in more traditional procedural coding styles would likely produce a morass of spaghetti code that would become difficult to develop in the first place, and impossible to maintain in the future. There are various programming techniques that can be utilized to help the developer produce a usable code base. One in particular, which you have already seen in this book, is the callback system. Sometimes the callback system is avoided because it is perceived as being "overkill" for the problem and requiring too much effort to implement your own. In many toolkits and languages, an existing callback implementation is restricted to a hardcoded set of events, leaving a developer high and dry for their own needs.

Matplotlib's callback system, however, is not restricted to any set of events. Developers are free to connect any callback function that takes a single argument to any arbitrarily named string. Developers are also free to issue any sort of arbitrarily named event, supplying their choice of an object for that event. This level of freedom is actually taken advantage of elsewhere in the library. The more intrepid reader may have noticed by now that the `Figure` class and the `Axes` class both have their own callback registry. No GUI-based events are processed through it, but it is useful for managing specialized events such as changes in the figure resolution, or changes in the limits of an axes. It is even used in certain kinds of artists to automatically trigger redraws when its data changes.

An event is triggered by a `CallbackRegistry` object through its `process()` method. This method takes two arguments: the name of the event to emit as a string and the event object to supply to the connected callback functions. The event argument can be anything. It does not have to inherit the `Event` class discussed earlier. This opens up a wide assortment of possibilities to the developer utilizing the callback design pattern.

Editor events

Let's now re-imagine our existing features as a set of events:

- Change frame
- Select storm
- Deselect storm
- Hide storm cells
- Delete storm cell
- Save storm data
- Display help

We will add two new methods to the `ControlSys` class: `_connect()` and `_emit()`. They are merely shorthand for the `mpl_connect()` command and the recently introduced `process()` method. In the constructor, we will connect some methods to the events we have just listed. In the case of the help method and the storm saving method, the methods originally supplied to the keymap will be connected to these two new events, and the keymap will instead merely call `_emit()` of the respective events. This can give a taste of fully customizable keymaps in the future. Meanwhile, this is what our constructor and the two new `_emit()` and `_connect()` methods now look like:

Source: `chp2/stormcell_editor2.py`

```python
class ControlSys(KeymapControl, PickControl):
    def __init__(self, fig, raddisp, data, polygons, stormdata):
        self.fig = fig
        self.raddisp = raddisp
        self.data = data
        self.i = 0
        self.selected = None
        self.polygons = polygons
        self.stormdata = stormdata
        self._hidekey = None
        self._hidecid = None
        KeymapControl.__init__(self, fig)
        PickControl.__init__(self, fig)

        self._connect('frame_change', self.update_radar_display)
        self._connect('frame_change', self.display_stormcells)
        self._connect('select', self.polygons.hilite_polygon)
        self._connect('deselect', self.polygons.lolite_polygon)
        self._connect('hide', self.polygons.toggle_polygons)
        self._connect('delete', self.polygons.delete_polygon)
        self._connect('delete', self.delete_stormcell)
        self._connect('save',
            lambda x: self.save_stormdata('polygons_new.shp'))
        self._connect('help', lambda x: self.display_help_menu())

        self.add_key_action('left', 'Back a frame',
                            lambda : self.change_frame(-1))
        self.add_key_action('right', 'Forward a frame',
                            lambda : self.change_frame(1))
        self.add_key_action('H', 'Hide polygons while holding',
                            self.enable_hide)
        self.add_key_action('d', 'Delete the selected stormcell',
                            self.delete_selected)
        self.add_key_action('w', 'Save the storm data',
                            lambda : self._emit('save', None))
        self.add_key_action('h', 'Display this help menu',
                            lambda : self._emit('help', None))
        self.add_pick_action(self.select_stormcell)

    def _emit(self, event, eventdata):
        self.fig.canvas.callbacks.process(event, eventdata)

    def _connect(self, event, callback):
        self.fig.canvas.mpl_connect(event, callback)
```

A significant amount of refactoring in the rest of the class has also taken place. Let's first take a look at the storm cell editing methods. The logic in delete_selected() method was split out into two parts, the deletion logic for the polygon artist, which we have seen in the Stormcells class, and the deletion logic for the storm cell data and its mapping. The delete_selected() method now only deals with managing the selection and emitting the delete action if appropriate. We also updated the saving method to accept a filename as an argument. The code is as follows:

Source: chp2/stormcell_editor2.py

```
def delete_selected(self):
    if self.selected is None:
        return
    # only delete when the selection is in the current frame
    if self.i != self.selected[0]:
        return

    self._emit('delete', self.selected)
    self.selected = None
    self.fig.canvas.draw_idle()

def delete_stormcell(self, inds):
    frame_i, cell_i = inds
    # Take it out of the raw stormdata object and everywhere else
    stormcell_index = self.stormmap[frame_i][cell_i]
    self.stormdata = np.delete(self.stormdata, stormcell_index)
    self.stormmap[frame_i] = np.delete(self.stormmap[frame_i],
                                       cell_i)
    # Also decrement any indexes greater than stormcell_index
    for indexes in self.stormmap:
        indexes[indexes > stormcell_index] -= 1

def save_stormdata(self, fname):
    storm_saver(fname, self.stormdata)
```

Next, the methods related to the display of the storms were refactored. In particular, the change_frame() method split out most of its logic into methods related to updating the radar display, which now resides in the RadarDisplay class, and methods related to updating the storm cell display. We begin to see the advantage of this design where we can logically compartmentalize portions of our interactive display. The radar display logic does not need to commingle with the polygon display logic or the storm cell selection logic. We can keep methods small and to the point, which makes them easier to work with. The code is as follows:

Source: chp2/stormcell_editor2.py

```python
def change_frame(self, frame_delta):
    newi = self.i + frame_delta
    if newi >= self.data.shape[0]:
        newi = self.data.shape[0] - 1
    if newi < 0:
        newi = 0
    if newi != self.i:
        self._emit('frame_change', newi)
        self.i = newi
        self.fig.canvas.draw_idle()

def update_radar_display(self, index):
    self.raddisp.update_display(self.data[index])

def display_stormcells(self, index):
    self.polygons.toggle_stormcells(self.i, False)
    self.polygons.toggle_stormcells(index, True)

def enable_hide(self):
    self.disconnect_keymap()
    self._hidekey = self._lastkey.lower()
    cid = self.fig.canvas.mpl_connect('key_release_event',
                                      self.release_hide)
    self._hidecid = cid
    self._emit('hide', self.i)
    self.fig.canvas.draw_idle()

def release_hide(self, event):
    key = event.key.lower()
    if key == self._hidekey and self._hidecid is not None:
        self.fig.canvas.mpl_disconnect(self._hidecid)
```

```
            self._hidekey = None
            self._hidecid = None
            self.connect_keymap()
            self.polygons.toggle_stormcells(self.i, True)
        self.fig.canvas.draw_idle()
```

Finally, the selection/deselection logic, which is contained entirely within the `select_stormcell()` method, has been significantly reduced in size with (just about) all display aspects removed from it. The method is now much easier to understand: deselect what was selected before, and select what has now been selected if it wasn't the same as before:

Source: `chp2/stormcell_editor2.py`

```
    def select_stormcell(self, event):
        if event.artist not in self.polygons.polygons:
            return
        ind = event.ind[0]
        self._emit('deselect', self.selected)
        if (self.i, ind) != self.selected:
            self.selected = (self.i, ind)
            self._emit('select', self.selected)
        else:
            self.selected = None
        self.fig.canvas.draw_idle()
```

Go ahead and give this program a try. You will find that it will behave exactly like before, with only an increase of approximately seventy lines of code. For those 70 lines of code, we have now broken down our `ControlSys` class full of methods that could only be used in an interactive context into a class where the majority of its code is now behind sensible methods and classes that do not care one bit about interactivity. This will become useful in the next chapter when we will need to produce animations of our display without being able to provide any manual inputs. This is also valuable for unit tests and also for building more complicated features that will need to reuse parts of the current code base.

Summary

We have come a long way in this chapter learning about the Matplotlib events and the built-in callback system. Our project application has grown in complexity significantly, requiring multiple refactors along the way. First, we connected to Matplotlib's GUI-based event system, particularly the key press and pick events. We also learned how to disconnect a callback function, both our own and Matplotlib's default keymap handler.

Then, you learned how to develop a more general keymap handler that even manages its own help documentation that could be produced on demand. After that, we added in a similar artist pick handler that allowed for different kinds of pickers to be used. With these two controllers working independently of each other, they were able to produce interactive features that they could not do on their own.

Next, we took a step back from our project and re-examined its goals as a storm track/cell editor. We examined the implications and the ease of conflating data and display. Bearing those lessons in mind, we reworked our application to achieve that separation and managed to round-trip data from an input file, through the editor, and saved them back out to a file that could then be used as input in the next run of the editor.

Finally, we took a deeper look at Matplotlib's callback system and realized just how flexible and generalized it was. With such a ready-to-use callback system available, we now have several application-specific events that are available for other functions to connect. This allowed us to split out the interactive-specific methods into more generalized noninteractive methods and reduce the amount of overlapping realms of responsibilities in the ever-growing `ControlSys` class.

In the next chapter, we will take advantage of this event-driven design to achieve a new feature with minimal amount of effort. We will be maximizing code reuse in developing animation code while also enhancing our interactive display. In the next chapter, we are going to Hollywood!

3
Animations

Animation can explain whatever the mind of man can conceive

- Walt Disney

More so than a static plot, an animation is innately interactive. It is much closer to how we take in the physical world, and therefore our minds can often assimilate its message in more meaningful ways. Another advantage of an animation is that it provides a convenient third dimension in which to display your data. So, rather than trying to cram all of your information into a single static plot you can spread out your data along this orthogonal axis, thereby reducing clutter. To put it another way, if a picture is worth a thousand words, then how many words must a whole movie of pictures be worth?

A short history

Prior to version 1.1 of **Matplotlib**, animations were often done hackishly. The implementations were usually GUI-specific and were often brittle. Things improved in version 1.0 with the introduction of a cross-platform `Timer` class, but the code examples in the gallery were an unsightly eyesore, completely in contrast to the typical easy reading of most Python code. On top of all that, there still wasn't any way to save the animations to movie formats, except to save each frame individually and use an external renderer to compose the movie.

Shortly after the release of version 1.0, Matplotlib contributor Ryan May created the animation module in order to complete a graduate course assignment without using MATLAB. This author collaborated with (recently) Dr. May in design reviews and shaking out the usual bugs that come with such fundamental additions to any library. He even used it for the same exact graduate course assignment the following year, finding additional room for improvements.

Unfortunately, as is the case for many contributions in the open source community, the module's documentation, while quite thorough in explaining its API, can hardly be used as a guide. This chapter probably represents the first complete guide to Matplotlib's animation module, showing all of the ins and outs and little tricks that I have developed over the past few years (surprising even Dr. May himself: "You did *what* with it?")

The fastest draw in the west

Your manager stops by your cubicle and says, "You know that track editor thing you have been working on? Yeah, I am going to need a movie of it that I can put it into a presentation for the Bobs by the end of the day. Mmm-kay? That would be great."

Don't freak out! Take a deep breath and think about it for a moment. At the end of the previous chapter, didn't we have something that looked a lot like an animation when pressing the arrow keys? All of the major code pieces are in place already. You just need something that can save the frames automatically, preferably right into an appropriate movie format. You don't have much time, so let's quickly jury-rig something for this one-off task and then worry about making it right later. Take the chp2/stormcell_editor2.py script we left off in the previous chapter and replace the final plt.show() function with the following few lines:

Source: chp3/quick_animation.py

```
from matplotlib.animation import FuncAnimation
anim = FuncAnimation(fig, lambda _: ctrl_sys.change_frame(1),
                     frames=data.shape[0], repeat=False)
anim.save('storms.gif', writer='imagemagick')
```

Assuming you have the powerful **ImageMagick** tool installed on your system, an image will be made for each frame of your animation and then combined into a single animated GIF file (and those individual frames will be cleaned up automatically). Provided the animation is short and simple, an animated GIF can be a very reliable format that can be used just about anywhere without worrying about the version of **PowerPoint**, **Impress**, or some other arcane presentation software (or then discovering that the computer in the lecture hall doesn't have just the right codec to play your movie). Of course, we will cover how to generate movies in other formats as well later in the chapter.

Run the script, view the GIF in a browser, and breath a sigh of relief. "That was easy", you think to yourself. "But, what exactly did I do?" Quite simply, the `FuncAnimation` class is one of the two types of `Animation` classes available in Matplotlib. It executes a given function for each frame. This function is expected to update some artists for a given frame index (which was the parameter that we choose to ignore for now with an underscore dummy variable in the lambda expression). We had `FuncAnimation` perform the same task as pressing the right arrow key a given number of times in the key map construction. We also specified that there would be no looping of the animation (which only really matters if we were going to display the animation rather than saving it). We then stated that the animation will be saved as `storms.gif` using the predefined ImageMagick animation writer settings. I bet you have never dreamed that an animation could be that easy?

The animation module

Now that we've had a crash course in animations for Matplotlib, let's take a step back and get to know the animation module. There is the base `Animation` class and three subclasses, namely, `TimedAnimation`, `FuncAnimation`, and `ArtistAnimation`. These classes handle all of the work necessary to initiate the animation upon call to `show()` and update the figure window with a new draw at the appropriate intervals. They also provide the interface to save your animation, hiding away many of the ugliness one might find when manually composing their own animation.

The most simple animation class is `ArtistAnimation`. You first perform all of the plotting, appending the artists of each frame into a list of lists. Each sublist represents all of the artists that should be visible for a given frame. The length of the list provided to the `ArtistAnimation` class is the number of frames the animation will have. When rendering, the `ArtistAnimation` class will modify the appropriate artists' visibility property and trigger a draw. This approach is the best way to handle simple, straightforward animation tasks.

To demonstrate the use of this class, let's grab the `Stormcells` class from the editing code at the end of the previous chapter. The `ArtistAnimation` class expects a list of lists, so we will build a one-element list containing the `PolyCollection` object for each frame, as follows:

Source: `chp3/stormcell_animation.py`

```
fig, ax = plt.subplots(1, 1)
stormcells = storm_loader('polygons.shp')
polycolls = Stormcells(ax, stormcells)
artists = [[p] for p in polycolls.polygons]
```

```
ax.autoscale(True)
ax.set_xlabel("Longitude")
ax.set_ylabel("Latitude")

anim = ArtistAnimation(fig, artists)
plt.show()
```

Run this script and a figure window will open up and show some polygons traveling across the plot area. Note that you still have the full default interactive navigation system available to you. You can zoom and pan this plot while the animation is played. Unfortunately, as of Matplotlib version 1.4, there are no built-in keymaps or GUI tools to control the animation such as play/pause or the speed of the animation. However, work is being done in version 2.1 to revamp the toolbar system to make it easier to add such features whenever an animation is added to a figure.

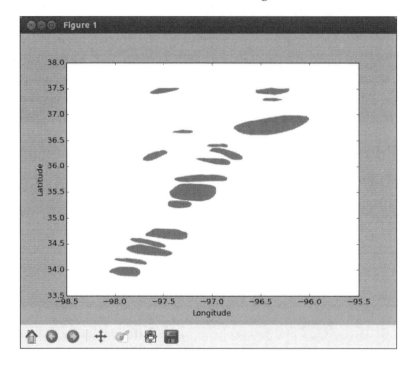

Storm cell polygon animation

One of the major downsides of ArtistAnimation is that it requires a separate instance of every artist in every frame. This can be very resource-intensive. For example, if we were to implement a radar loop as an ArtistAnimation class, not only would the radar data be held in memory for the entire time series, but also the RGBA image data for each frame. This becomes impractical for large animations. Another downside is that it requires all artists to be made a priori, thereby precluding use cases such as dynamic content or the cogeneration of a movie and the data via a simulation. And so, the FuncAnimation class can be used instead. The idea with this class is that you provide a function that will be responsible to modify artists prior to rendering each frame. So, for example, your animation function for an image animation could load image data into the memory one frame at a time (similar to how we do it right now with our radar viewer). In fact, let's take the RadarDisplay class we created in the storm cell editor as the start:

Source: chp3/radar_animation.py

```
ncf = netcdf_file('KTLX_20100510_22Z.nc')
data = ncf.variables['Reflectivity']
lats = ncf.variables['lat']
lons = ncf.variables['lon']

fig, ax = plt.subplots(1, 1)
raddisp = RadarDisplay(ax, lats, lons)
raddisp.update_display(data[0])
cb = fig.colorbar(raddisp.im)
cb.set_label("Reflectivity (dBZ)")
ax.set_xlabel("Longitude")
ax.set_ylabel("Latitude")

anim = FuncAnimation(fig,
    lambda idx: raddisp.update_display(data[idx]),
    frames=data.shape[0], repeat=False)
plt.show()
```

There are only two new lines—the import of FuncAnimation (not shown) and its instantiation prior to show(). Unlike ArtistAnimation, this type of animation needs to have some way of knowing how many frames the animation has, hence the frames argument. The function supplied to the constructor should accept a frame index for its first argument. There is a mechanism to supply other arguments to this function, but we will discuss this later. When you run this script, a figure window will pop up and a radar loop will play.

A common pitfall with first time users of animations is that they do not save the instantiated object to a variable. This is understandable as Matplotlib users tend to get used to not saving the output of calls, such as `plt.imshow()` and `ax.scatter()`, without any consequence. Plotting works fine with functions such as these because the returned objects are automatically added to the appropriate axes object, which is, in turn, recorded in the appropriate figure object. This is, in turn, recorded in what is known as the "Pyplot State Machine". A Matplotlib user can go quite far having never saved a single artist object into a variable. This is because the pyplot state machine keeps those objects "alive" and therefore these objects are not garbage collected. Up to at least version 1.4, animation objects are not automatically saved anywhere and would typically be garbage-collected shortly after instantiation, if not stored in a variable.

Any animation based off of the `TimedAnimation` class, which the previously mentioned classes are, have some constructor arguments to control the timing of the animation. By default, the animation is timed to advance a frame every 200 milliseconds. This can be modified by the `interval` argument. An additional delay can also be added to the last frame of the animation loop prior to restarting the loop (also in milliseconds). Such a delay, provided by the `repeat_delay` argument, often helps users gain an easy visual cue for the start and end of an animation. By default, there is no additional delay. Of course, one could also decide not to even have a loop in the first place by setting the `repeat` argument to `False`.

Advanced animations

So far, we have seen how to inject animations into an existing Matplotlib application as if it was an afterthought. This is perfectly valid, but what if we spend time considering how best to prepare our codebase for animation use? What sort of features and effects could we enable?

Your manager drops by and says, "You know the animation I showed the Bobs the other day? They need one with the tracks displayed, mmm-kay? We need to push this, so I am going to need you to come in on Saturday to get this done, that would be great." It is a good thing we had the foresight to isolate our display elements into their own classes in the previous chapter. Now, it is just a matter of adding a new display element, that is, tracks! We will model this one closely to the `Stormcells` design, but there are going to be some fundamental differences. First, the storm cells are organized by frames while the tracks are not. This leads to a bit of a complication for the purposes of animations. The storm tracks will need to grow longer with time as opposed to being discrete sets of artists for each frame. Let's first take a look at how one can implement a `Tracks` class:

Source: chp3/quick_animation2.py

```python
class Tracks(object):
    def __init__(self, ax):
        self.tracks = None
        self.initialize_lines(ax)

    @staticmethod
    def create_trackmap(stormdata):
        trackmap = []
        for trackid in range(np.max(stormdata['track_id']) + 1):
            indexes = np.where(stormdata['track_id'] ==
                               trackid)[0]
            # Ensure the track segments are in chronological order
            seg_indxs = np.argsort(stormdata['frame_index'][indexes])
            trackmap.append(indexes[seg_indxs])
        return trackmap

    def remove_lines(self):
        if self.tracks is not None:
            self.tracks.remove()
            self.tracks = None

    def initialize_lines(self, ax):
        self.remove_lines()
        self.tracks = LineCollection([])
        ax.add_collection(self.tracks)

    def update_lines(self, frame_index, stormdata):
        segments = []
        for indexes in self.create_trackmap(stormdata):
            trackdata = stormdata[indexes]
            trackdata = trackdata[trackdata['frame_index'] <=
                                  frame_index]
            # must always be something in a track, even NaNs.
            segments.append(zip(trackdata['xcent'],
                                trackdata['ycent'])
                            or [(np.nan, np.nan)])
        self.tracks.set_segments(segments)

    def lolite_line(self, indx):
        self.hilite_line(indx, 1)
```

```
def hilite_line(self, indx, lw=4):
    if indx is not None:
        lws = self.tracks.get_linewidths()
        lws[indx] = lw
        self.tracks.set_linewidths(lws)
```

Much like the `RadarDisplay` class, we will initialize an `Artist` object (in this case, `LineCollection`) with no data in it. This way, we have an artist object to add to the axes from the start and then we would never need to concern ourselves about the axes again. Therefore, subsequent frame draws will compute which points will be visible and set them as line segments for each available track. Any tracks that are yet to form by the time of `frame_index` will instead be represented by a single set of **Not a Number (NaN)**, which Matplotlib always renders as a blank.

Similar to the `Stormcells` class, we will have a method that can generate a "track map" that would index the raw data by tracks and be used to build up the track lines. One may express concern with the inefficiency that would arise with repeatedly computing the track map with every frame update rather than simply reusing the track map from some other source. The answer to this point is to avoid the trap of premature optimization. This interface design is very simple to use and it is relatively easy to understand. We can always add optimizations later if we find that they are warranted.

Some additions were made to the `ControlSys` constructor, particularly the addition of a `lines` instance to the class and the connecting of an `update_track_display()` method to the `'frame_change'` event.

Finally, let's see what the main logic has become:

Source: `chp3/quick_animation2.py`

```
if __name__ == '__main__':
    from matplotlib.animation import FuncAnimation

    ncf = netcdf_file('KTLX_20100510_22Z.nc')
    data = ncf.variables['Reflectivity']
    lats = ncf.variables['lat']
    lons = ncf.variables['lon']
    stormcells = storm_loader('polygons.shp')

    fig, ax = plt.subplots(1, 1)
    raddisp = RadarDisplay(ax, lats, lons)
    raddisp.update_display(data[0])
    cb = fig.colorbar(raddisp.im)
    polycolls = Stormcells(ax, stormcells)
    linecoll = Tracks(ax)
```

```
# Turn on the first frame's polygons
polycolls.toggle_polygons(0, True)
ax.autoscale(True)

ctrl_sys = ControlSys(fig, raddisp, data, polycolls, linecoll,
                      stormcells)
cb.set_label("Reflectivity (dBZ)")
ax.set_xlabel("Longitude")
ax.set_ylabel("Latitude")

anim = FuncAnimation(fig, lambda _: ctrl_sys.change_frame(1),
                     frames=data.shape[0], repeat=False)
anim.save('storms_with_tracks.gif', writer='imagemagick')
```

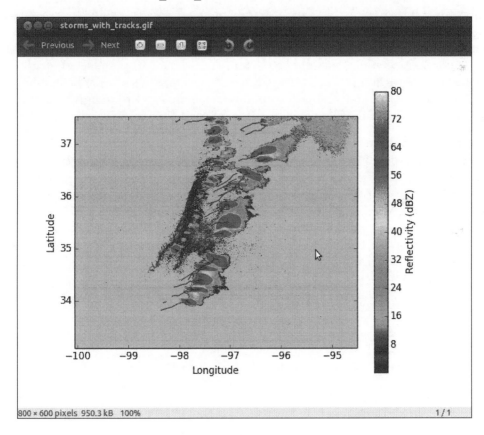

Viewing the GIF animation of the storm cells with trailing tracks using an image viewer

Go ahead and run this script and send off the `storms_with_tracks.gif` animation to your manager. You can now see how careful consideration during development can make it fairly simple to add features such as animated storm tracks because all of the pieces are in their logical places. We can also see how relatively easy it would be to add and remove display elements to and from `ControlSys`. Also, as will soon be demonstrated, we can easily mix and match these display elements for other purposes.

Oh, and feel free not to come in on Saturday now that we have this done.

Event source

Animations in Matplotlib are event-driven from a source object that handles callbacks. This seemingly simple object is actually critical for properly timed animations in Matplotlib. Think about it for a moment. In order for callbacks to be triggered on a regular interval, the time must be checked frequently. If Matplotlib were to perform this time check itself while the figure window is displayed, then the GUI's event loop would constantly be interrupted, which would cause all sorts of performance issues and responsiveness problems. So, timings need to be handled by the GUI. This is why older Matplotlib animation examples were so ugly and difficult to share. They often had GUI-specific tricks to achieve the timing effect desired.

By default, the `TimedAnimation` objects will create an event source object that ties into the GUI's timing features. This makes the creation of a single animation very easy and intuitive for users. However, what if you have multiple animation objects that you want to use together in a single plot? While all of our examples so far have had a single `Animation` instance with possibly many components, there is no reason why one could not have multiple `Animation` instances, provided that the developer takes some care in juggling them. Let's take the three classes we made in the previous example and create an animation object for each of them and run them all at once. Here is the main logic:

Source: `chp3/simultaneous_animations.py`

```
if __name__ == '__main__':
    stormcells = storm_loader('polygons.shp')
    ncf = netcdf_file('KTLX_20100510_22Z.nc')
    data = ncf.variables['Reflectivity']
    lats = ncf.variables['lat']
    lons = ncf.variables['lon']
    framecnt = data.shape[0]

    fig, ax = plt.subplots(1, 1)
```

```
rad_disp = RadarDisplay(ax, lats, lons)
cb = fig.colorbar(rad_disp.im)
trks = Tracks(ax)
cells = Stormcells(ax, stormcells)
cells.toggle_stormcells(0, True)

cb.set_label("Reflectivity (dBZ)")
ax.set_xlabel("Longitude")
ax.set_ylabel("Latitude")

radanim = FuncAnimation(fig,
    lambda i, dat: rad_disp.update_display(dat[i]),
    framecnt, fargs=(data,))
trkanim = FuncAnimation(fig, trks.update_lines,
                        framecnt, fargs=(stormcells,))
strmanim = ArtistAnimation(fig, [[p] for p in cells.polygons])

plt.show()
```

Nothing out of the ordinary here. We even demonstrate how to pass additional arguments to our update function in the respective `FuncAnimation` objects via the `fargs` parameter. Previously, the `ControlSys` method passed into the `FuncAnimation` constructor already had access to these other pieces of data, but since the `Track` and `RadarDisplay` objects are designed not to carry any of the raw data, this information would need to be supplied externally via the `fargs` argument in the `FuncAnimation` constructor.

Now run the preceding script. You should notice that something seems... off. Looking closely, you may see that the radar display and the polygons are not updating at quite the same time. The animation looks stuttered and unsynchronized. This is because each of the three animation objects created here have their own `event_source` instance, each of which will be started independently of each other, and each will cause their own draw calls. Luckily, there is a simple solution to this problem:

Source: chp3/synchronized_animations.py

```
radanim = FuncAnimation(fig,
    lambda i, dat: rad_disp.update_display(dat[i]),
    framecnt, fargs=(data,))
event_source = radanim.event_source
trkanim = FuncAnimation(fig, trks.update_lines,
                        framecnt, fargs=(stormcells,),
                        event_source=event_source)
strmanim = ArtistAnimation(fig, [[p] for p in cells.polygons],
                           event_source=event_source)
```

What we have done is take the first animation's `event_source` object and supply it to the other two animation instances. Now, all three animations will be running off of the same timer. Running this new script, you should see a much more coherent, synchronized animation than in the previous example.

Timers

Most of the time, you will never need to interact directly with a timer object. The animations manage it all for you. However, timers are completely independent of the animation module. Therefore, it is entirely possible to use timers for animation-like effects in your interactive applications. Oftentimes, such effects can add a bit of a "wow" factor to an otherwise boring feature. Sometimes, features such as transitions can provide important visual cues to the user or unobtrusively convey subtle information about what the application is doing. Consider, for example, the age-old "spinning hourglass" mouse cursor to indicate that the application is busy (or the "spinning beach ball" for Mac OS X users). By being animated as opposed to just a static image, it helps convey to the user that work is progressing and that the system is not entirely frozen.

Our application does not have any busy cycles, so we aren't going to add any spinning beach balls. However, let's consider a feature to jump ahead several frames with a single press of a key. This is a convenient function that can help a user jump quickly through a longer radar sequence. We can easily implement this by connecting the up and down arrow keys to call `change_frames()` with the values -5 and 5, respectively. However, the user would miss out on seeing any frames in between because the display will just jump to the requested frame. Instead, let's implement a frame transition feature that will use a timer to quickly hop through the frames:

```
def frame_hop(self, frame_delta):
    def hopper(ctrl_sys, increm, final):
        ctrl_sys.change_frame(increm)
        if increm > 0 and ctrl_sys.i >= final:
            return False
        elif increm < 0 and ctrl_sys.i <= final:
            return False

    increm = np.sign(frame_delta)
    if increm > 0:
        final = min(self.i+frame_delta, self.data.shape[0]-1)
    else:
        final = max(0, self.i + frame_delta)
    timer = self.fig.canvas.new_timer(100)
    timer.add_callback(hopper, self, increm, final)
    timer.start()
```

A new method was added to the `ControlSys`. This creates a one-off callback function called `hopper()` that calls the `change_frame()` method with a positive or negative delta. The callback then checks whether it has now reached its destination frame, and if so, removes the callback by returning `False`. A return of `False` (as opposed to `None` or zero or anything that would inadvertently evaluate to `False`) is a mechanism by which a callback can remove itself from the timer. After creating the callback function, the `frame_hop()` method then computes what the destination frame would be, taking into account the bounds of the radar sequence. Then, a new timer object, which is associated with the canvas, is created. Its callback interval is set to `100` milliseconds. Next, the `hopper()` callback is added to the timer along with its three arguments. Finally, the timer is started. Of course, we will need to add the appropriate keys to the keymap:

```
self.add_key_action('up', 'Back 5 frames',
                    lambda : self.frame_hop(-5))
self.add_key_action('down', 'Forward 5 frames',
                    lambda : self.frame_hop(5))
```

The timer is asynchronous, so the application will continue just fine after `start()` is called. A tenth of a second later, the callback is triggered, causing the display to step a single frame. A tenth of a second later, the callback is triggered again. All this while, the application is still responsive to any other interactive features. Finally, after triggering the callback the appropriate number of times, the callback function will terminate the timer by returning `False` and all of the frame-hopping components are cleaned up automatically.

Run the script we saw before for implementing a frame transition feature and use the up and down arrow keys along with your right and left keys to change frames. The display will hop along the radar sequence with only a single key press. Note that not even a single `Animation` instance was used to achieve this effect. Being able to directly utilize a timer in your application can gain you very fine-grained control over your application, which you might not be able to achieve with an `Animation` object. The advantage of an `Animation` object is for when you don't already have the framework in place to perform the desired animation action (we already had the `change_frame()` method), and it provides the mechanism to save the animations. The ability to save animations will be discussed in depth shortly.

Blitting

Blitting is a technique where anything in the animation that is static will only be drawn once and treated as a background for any animated artists. It is an age-old optimization that can significantly reduce the amount of work needed to render each frame. Back in the days when processing power was a premium, any sort of optimization was valuable to improve the smoothness of an animation (the technique wholly predates Matplotlib). It was also a relatively easy optimization to understand and implement, so it worked its way into the vernacular of programmers who do not regularly deal with animations.

So matplolib has the ability to handle blitting across most of the interactive backends; the Mac OS X backend does not support it due to limitations in Matplotlib's design. It is often misunderstood, however, and so it is turned off by default (plus, this is the mode that achieves full compatibility across all backends). In most situations, on even moderate hardware of the past few years, you will not notice the difference between blitting and not blitting. Indeed, one should treat blitting like one would for any other optimization technique—it is good to know about, but don't prematurely optimize your code until you determine that you need it. Blitting can cause enough headaches for even the most experienced users, so you would only want to deal with it if you absolutely have to. For a technique that is conceptually simple, it can be surprisingly tricky to use.

The first thing to remember about blitting is that it is extremely difficult to use if you have multiple animation objects in play. This is because the first step of blitting is to store an unanimated image in memory that would serve as the static background. If multiple animation objects are in play, you have no guarantee that another animation has already performed a draw when your blitting animation object captures that initial blit. Second, panning and zooming may not work properly for blitting. Considering that the drawing of the ticks and labels tend to be the most expensive of the typically static parts of the plot draw, blitting without the ticks and labels tend to be fairly pointless. Future versions of Matplotlib may contain fixes for this limitation, allowing full interactivity during blitting as well as providing possible optimizations to the axis ticking system so that refreshes to the axis ticks are not as expensive as they are now.

Finally, z-order is not respected during blitting. You cannot have a static component in front of an animated component. This becomes particularly evident in the case of annotations and legends. Without blitting, an animated component will get drawn behind a legend or any annotation. However, during blitting, legends and annotations are considered to be static and will be drawn as a background for the animated components.

Blitting with `ArtistAnimation` instances is simple because all of the animated components are controlled by the animation instance. Just pass a `blit=True` keyword argument to the constructor. Blitting with the more advanced `FuncAnimation` class can be trickier. One thing we haven't covered yet about the animation functions is what they should return. Our examples have them return nothing at all, which is perfectly fine to do if you are not blitting. However, when the `blit` property has been set to `True`, your animation function will need to return a list of all the animated `Artist` objects for that particular frame. This way, the blitting code will know exactly which artists it needs to clear from the image (as opposed to normal animations, which draws each frame from scratch). Without the returned list of `Artists` by the animation function, blitting will not work.

Observant readers may have noticed another interesting argument to the `FuncAnimation` constructor — `init_func`. This function, if given, is to draw the **clear frame** of the animation. The clear frame of an animation is typically the static background of the animation, but it isn't restricted to just the static components, as it can return a list of animated artists. Besides, when starting the animation, the clear frame is drawn whenever the blit image needs to be refreshed, such as when the figure window is resized. The `init_func` function is called with no arguments, not even any supplied `fargs` parameter. If no `init_func` is provided, then the first full frame of the animation, sans any returned `Artists`, is used instead. So, resizing the figure window while playing a `FuncAnimation` that does not have an `init_func` argument will result in restarting the animation sequence.

Recipes

There are a few commonly requested animation effects that pop up on Matplotlib's mailing list. Unfortunately, it isn't really possible to generalize them into a set of utility functions that can be included into Matplotlib. Instead, like a chef, you will need to figure out how to best achieve the effect that you want within your masterpiece. We can provide some basic examples to demonstrate some concepts.

Tails

When showing moving particles, having a trailing track behind the particle helps to visualize the motion. This is essentially what we implemented in the previous section. However, what if the time series is very long or if there are many particles to visualize? Keeping all of these very long tails around indefinitely can make for a very busy scene. What if we snipped these tails? Let's modify the code for synchronizing animations in the *Event Source* section of this chapter by updating the `Track` class and showing just the tracks as an animation:

Source: chp3/track_tails.py

```
class Tracks(object):
    def __init__(self, ax, tails=None):
        self.tracks = None
        self.tails = tails
        self.initialize_lines(ax)

    ...

    def update_lines(self, frame_index, stormdata):
        segments = []
        for indexes in self.create_trackmap(stormdata):
            trackdata = stormdata[indexes]
            trackdata = trackdata[trackdata['frame_index'] <=
                                  frame_index]
            if self.tails:
                mask = (trackdata['frame_index'] >=
                        (frame_index - self.tails))
                trackdata = trackdata[mask]
            # must always be something in a track, even NaNs.
            segments.append(zip(trackdata['xcent'],
                                trackdata['ycent'])
                            or [(np.nan, np.nan)])
        self.tracks.set_segments(segments)
```

We build a boolean mask to index each track's segments that are to be visible. The main logic only has a tiny change:

```
if __name__ == '__main__':
    stormcells = storm_loader('polygons.shp')
    fig, ax = plt.subplots(1, 1)
    trks = Tracks(ax, 3)
    ax.set_xlim(stormcells['xcent'].min(), stormcells['xcent'].max())
    ax.set_ylim(stormcells['ycent'].min(), stormcells['ycent'].max())
    ax.set_xlabel("Longitude")
    ax.set_ylabel("Latitude")
    trkanim = FuncAnimation(fig, trks.update_lines,
            stormcells['frame_index'].max() + 1,
            fargs=(stormcells,))
    plt.show()
```

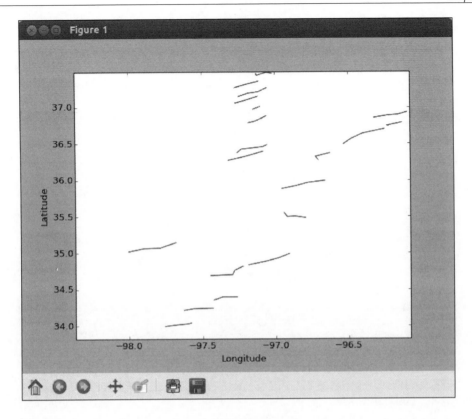

A storm track tail animation

When you run this example, you will see short lines "crawling" about the plot area. The lines are at most three segments long, as parameterized in the `Tracks` constructor. This is just one approach to line tailing. Another involves simple slicing of the NumPy array containing the vertexes (for example, `verts[-tail:]`). A word to the wise, though. Do watch out for tail parameters of zero when slicing like this. A negative zero is still zero, and as such, would result in an array slice that goes from the first element to the end rather than an empty slice.

Fades

Having artist objects fade with time is another popular animation effect. Much like the tails, fades help us give a sense of past information, which can easily be compared against current information. Let's again modify the code for synchronizing animations in the *Event Source* section of this chapter, but this time keeping only the Stormcells class and showing just the storm cells as an animation with faded polygons trailing behind the current polygons:

Source: chp3/stormcell_fade.py

```python
if __name__ == '__main__':
    stormcells = storm_loader('polygons.shp')
    frameCnt = stormcells['frame_index'].max() + 1

    fig, ax = plt.subplots(1, 1)
    cells = Stormcells(ax, stormcells)
    ax.autoscale(True)

    polys = [p for p in cells.polygons]
    for p in polys:
        p.set_visible(True)
        p.set_alpha(0.0)

    def update(frame, polys):
        for i, p in enumerate(polys):
            alpha = 0.0 if i > frame else 1.0 / ((frame - i + 1)**2)
            p.set_alpha(alpha)

    ax.set_xlabel("Longitude")
    ax.set_ylabel("Latitude")
    strmanim = FuncAnimation(fig, update, frameCnt,
                             fargs=(polys,))
    plt.show()
```

When this script is run, it shows the following output:

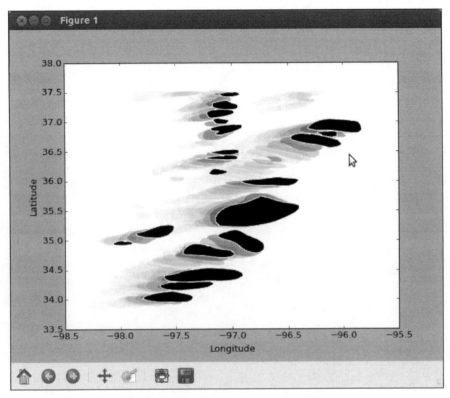

Animated "fades" of the storm cell polygons

Unlike storm tracks, polygons were previously set up to use the `ArtistAnimation` class. However, because of the simplicity of that animator, one cannot apply effects such as tails and fades (unless all such instances were previously rendered). Instead, for just about any effect, one would need to use `FuncAnimation`. So, for this example, we will need to initially set all polygons to be visible, but with full transparency. This way, you don't show any of the polygons in that quick moment between the `plt.show()` command and the first frame's update. Then, we create a little function that will compute the transparency level for all polygons based upon the current frame. The alpha value will be one for the polygons in the current frame, zero for the polygons in any future frames, and the value rapidly approaching zero the further back in time one goes.

Saving animations

While having a quick and easy way of displaying an animation is nice, you would likely need to save the animation somehow. The animation module provides the "writer" framework that allows multiple movie-writing mechanisms to be available to users. One of them that you have already seen is the simple frame-saving mechanism that is fed into ImageMagick to convert frames into an animated GIF. Three additional mechanisms are packaged with Matplotlib, namely, 'ffmpeg', 'avconv', and 'mencoder'. Actually, there are four more, but they are essentially slightly modified versions of the three and 'imagemagick'. These three writers provide interfaces to their respective encoding tools. The avconv tool is a somewhat recent fork of the popular ffmpeg tool from libav, so they are quite similar for now, while the mencoder tool is the encoder put out by the same people that release the popular "mplayer" application.

While these writer classes are packaged with Matplotlib, the tools themselves are not (neither is ImageMagick). If you attempt to save an animation using a tool that is not installed, you will get an error. So, make sure you have installed one of these tools and set your animation.writer setting in your matplotlibrc file that we discussed in *Chapter 1, Introducing Interactive Plotting*. Here is a snippet from my own rc file, where ffmpeg is used by default:

```
###ANIMATION settings
animation.writer : ffmpeg       # MovieWriter 'backend' to use
animation.codec : mpeg4         # Codec to use for writing movie
animation.bitrate: -1           # Controls size/quality tradeoff
                                #for movie.
                                # -1 implies let utility auto-
                                #determine
animation.frame_format: 'png'   # Controls frame format used by temp
                                #files
animation.ffmpeg_path: 'ffmpeg' # Path to ffmpeg binary. Without
                                #full path
                                # $PATH is searched
animation.ffmpeg_args: ''       # Additional arguments to pass
                                #to mencoder
```

Notes about codecs and file formats

While I will not claim to possess anything more than a passing familiarity with movie formats, I recognize that neither do many other people. For those who have had experience editing and creating movies and understand these concepts far more extensively, you can skip this section; be assured that I could not possibly add any new knowledge. For those reading on, there are likely to be some over-simplifications. As such, this section is only intended to provide enough information to successfully render animations and avoid pitfalls and should not be considered authoritative.

A codec is a library that will code and decode a video (or audio) data stream. Some common video codecs are Theora, DivX, and H.264 (also known as MPEG-4). Most movie writers can utilize a wide variety of codecs. How the video stream is encoded is separate from the movie format, often called the "container" format. It is called a container format because it contains not only the encoded video stream, but also the audio stream, the metadata, subtitles, and anything else that might be with the movie file. With many movie writers, the container format is automatically determined from the specified filename extension. Some common container formats are OGG (.ogg), AVI (.avi), and MPEG (.mpg or .mpeg).

Not all codecs are compatible with all kinds of container formats, and not all containers can be produced by all of the movie writers. Take care in choosing an appropriate combination of codec, writer, and container format for your saved animations. It is entirely possible to produce invalid movie files. The Matplotlib library will not know that a specified combination is invalid, so will not produce a warning or an error. One particular invalid combination that has always confused me is using the 'ffmpeg' writer with the 'mpeg4' codec and a file with a .mpg or .mpeg extension. This will not produce a valid animation because the MPEG container format is older than the MP4 codec and not compatible. However, the file will be valid if you set the filename extension to .avi or .mp4.

Another factor to consider while saving your animations is how you plan to display them. If you are just going to view the files yourself on the same system that recorded the animation, then it shouldn't be an issue. If your system can write the animation, then it can play the animation. However, quite often, the purpose of saving the animation is to share it with others. This means that their playback abilities will need to be considered.

I've made attempts to figure out an ideal default configuration for Matplotlib's animations, aiming for the widest platform compatibility possible, as opposed to focusing upon compression and quality. At this time, only one combination could be found that could play on stock installations of OpenOffice Impress on Mac OS X, Microsoft Office PowerPoint on Windows / Mac OS X, QuickTime player on Mac OS X, and LibreOffice on Linux. It is possible to play just about any of these videos on any of these systems with additional tools and add-ons installed, but what was tested were stock installations. Refer to the following table to check the compatibility of the different combinations of codecs and containers with various display and presentation software on different platforms:

Codec	Format	OpenOffice Impress (Mac OS X)	MS Office PowerPoint (Mac OS X)	QuickTime (Mac OS X)	LibreOffice Impress (Linux)	MS Office PowerPoint (Windows)
mpeg4	.mp4	✓	✓	✓	✓	✗
	.avi	✗	✗	✗	✓	✓
	.mov	✓	✓	✓	✓	✗
	.m4v	✗	✗	✗	✓	✗
	.asf	✗	✗	✓	✓	✗
libtheora	.avi	✗	✗	✗	✓	✗
	.mov	✗	✗	✗	✗	✗
	.m4v	✗	✗	✗	✗	✗
	.asf	✗	✗	✗	✓	✗
msmpeg4	.avi	✗	✗	✗	✓	✓
	.mov	✗	✗	✗	✗	✗
	.m4v	✗	✗	✗	✗	✗
	.asf	✗	✗	✗	✓	✓
msmpeg4v2	.avi	✗	✓	✓	✓	✓
	.mov	✗	✗	✗	✗	✓
	.m4v	✗	✗	✗	✗	✗
	.asf	✗	✗	✓	✓	✓
wmv1	.avi	✗	✓	✓	✓	✓
	.mov	✗	✗	✗	✗	✗
	.m4v	✗	✗	✗	✗	✗
	.asf	✗	✗	✓	✓	✓
wmv2	.avi	✗	✓	✓	✓	✓
	.mov	✗	✗	✗	✗	✗

Codec	Format	OpenOffice Impress (Mac OS X)	MS Office PowerPoint (Mac OS X)	QuickTime (Mac OS X)	LibreOffice Impress (Linux)	MS Office PowerPoint (Windows)
	.m4v	✗	✗	✗	✗	✗
	.asf	✗	✗	✓	✓	✓

While this is not exhaustive, it should provide good guidance to help users select what kind of movie file they need for their uses. There are many other possible combinations that were not tested, so an ideal combination may yet to be discovered. Your best bet for cross-platform compatibility is to use the default codec of mpeg4 in a .mp4 container.

Simultaneous animations

Earlier in this chapter, we showed how easy it was to use multiple independent (but synchronized) animation objects. This is often ideal for producing well-modularized code. For example, one may wish to reuse the radar display portion of the code for synchronizing animations in the *Event Source* section of this chapter for a separate app without any of the storm tracks or polygons. One could then even mix and match animations from other sources for new and interesting applications.

This is all good for displaying purposes, but what about saving the animations? Animation saving is initiated from an animation object rather than some other parent object of the animations, and doing so would only step through that particular animation, leaving any other animations unaware that anything is going on. To address this problem, the extra_anim keyword argument is available in the save() method. This argument expects a list of other animation objects that are all attached to the same figure. Let's modify the code for synchronizing animations in the *Event Source* section of this chapter to include an animation-saving step:

Source: chp3/saving_multi_animations.py

```
radanim = FuncAnimation(fig,
    lambda i, dat: rad_disp.update_display(dat[i]),
    framecnt, fargs=(data,))
event_source = radanim.event_source
trkanim = FuncAnimation(fig, trks.update_lines,
                        framecnt, fargs=(stormcells,),
                        event_source=event_source)
strmanim = ArtistAnimation(fig, [[p] for p in cells.polygons],
                        event_source=event_source)
radanim.save('multi_animation.mp4',
            extra_anim=[trkanim, strmanim])
plt.show()
```

It doesn't matter which animation object gets used to call `save()`. Therefore, a coding style that I tend to employ is to build a list of animation objects and invoke the first animation object's `save()` method and pass in a slice of the rest:

```
if anims:
    anims[0].save(fname, extra_anim=anims[1:])
```

This is particularly useful for applications where the animation elements are configurable. Also notice in our example that we were still able to call `plt.show()` after saving the animation. This is much like how one should call `plt.show()` after saving an image, not before. If you want to do both animation saving and animation showing, then the `save()` must occur prior to `show()`.

How animations are saved

Most of the time, there will be no need to concern yourself with the particulars of how Matplotlib saves animations. However, it can easily get confusing trying to debug a problem, so having a familiarity with it will grant you insight into how to hunt down your bug. Furthermore, with this knowledge, you will be able to create your own custom writer classes for specialized purposes.

First, while the `Animation` objects provide a `save()` method, it is merely for convenience and does not mean that the animation performs any saving; however, it does an important housekeeping task besides argument sanitation and loading up default configurations. The animation must first disconnect itself from drawing event notifications. This is to prevent accidental triggering of the animation's event source (typically, the timer). After the saving is complete, it will need to reconnect itself to the draw notification system. This allows you to `show()` the animation after saving it.

For the process of saving an animation (or multiple simultaneous animations, as we just demonstrated in the previous section), the `save()` method enters a `with` clause, calling the animation writer's `saving()` context manager. This context manager performs any necessary actions to `setup()` and `finish()` the animation-saving process, such as establishing subprocess pipes to the chosen encoder program. Within the context clause, frames are iteratively obtained from the animation's `new_saved_frame_seq()` method, stepping through them without a timer. After obtaining a frame, the writer's `grab_frame()` method is called, which essentially calls `savefig()` on the animation's figure object, passing the frames along to the encoder.

`Animation` objects in Matplotlib have the ability to keep around a copy of the frame sequence. This is particularly useful for animation loops. For `FuncAnimation` objects, for example, the supplied frame count doesn't need to be an integer. It can be any iterable sequence, which would get supplied to the animation function instead of the frame index. Therefore, the `Animation` object cannot assume that it can go back to the beginning of the input sequence when it is looping the animation. For `FuncAnimation` objects, frames are cached as they are drawn interactively because there is no guarantee that the frames could be regenerated. Therefore, the "frame sequence" is a counter for the first pass through the animation, but then it can also be a sequence of rendered frames for subsequent passes. So, depending upon the type of input and the `Animation` subclass, the `new_saved_frame_seq()` method will provide a fresh iterator for the (possibly cached) frame sequence. For basic `TimedAnimation` objects, this is merely a call to its `new_frame_seq()` method.

Session recorder

Your manager drops by your cubicle and says, "Yeah, so, uhm, this storm track editor you are working on, the Bobs want to be able to record themselves using the application, mmm-kay? So, why don't you go ahead and just slip in that feature there, making a video just like you did before?"

So, the Bobs want the ability to record an interactive session. To them, this is just a tiny difference from what you have done before. To you, this is a fundamentally different problem. First of all, the animations you have made so far have all been driven by timers rather than by a user. Second of all, you haven't tried saving an animation during a live interactive session. Is it even possible? Doesn't the `save()` method wait until the animation is completed, preventing the execution of any other code? How would any of the interactive features work while the `save()` method is keeping Matplotlib out of the event loop?

These are all very valid questions and highlights fundamental limitations of Matplotlib's animations and writers. However, not all is lost! The roadblock to overcome is the fact that the `save()` method is synchronous. If we could make it asynchronous, then we could get somewhere with this.

Remember in the previous section, the `save()` method used a context to set up and tear down the animation-saving process. Also, within the context, the frame sequence is processed in a `for` loop, recording each frame. With a session recorder, there is no frame sequence to iterate over, so let's create a subclass of `TimedAnimation` that will return an iterator to an empty list. Furthermore, we need an animation writer class that will not stop writing the animation just because the iteration stopped like this:

Source: `chp3/session_recorder.py`

```
from matplotlib.animation import TimedAnimation, MencoderWriter

class SessionAnimation(TimedAnimation):
    def new_frame_seq(self):
        return iter([])

class SessionWriter(MencoderWriter):
    def finish(self):
        pass
```

We created a special `TimedAnimation` subclass that will always return an empty frame sequence, and we subclassed `MencoderWriter` so that we could turn its `finish()` method into a no-op. This would allow for the `save()` method to become asynchronous. You can also similarly subclass `FFMpegWriter`, `AVConvWriter`, or `ImageMagickWriter`, as they operate under similar principles. However, for any of the file-based writers, such as `ImageMagickFileWriter` and `FFMpegFileWriter`, the `finish()` method is supposed to execute the encoding step, and so their `cleanup()` methods would need to be jury-rigged to perform that action along with its usual cleanup step.

Of course, these lines by themselves wouldn't be enough to create a session recorder. How could we wield these two classes to get what we need? While the `SessionAnimation` class does not have any frames to provide, it is still a timer-based animator, and as such, comes with a timer. We can leverage this timer to attach a callback that would trigger the writer object's `grab_frame()` method:

Source: `chp3/session_recorder.py`

```
from contextlib import contextmanager
from matplotlib import rcParams
import matplotlib.pyplot as plt

@contextmanager
def record_session(filename, interval=100, codec=None,
                   bitrate=None, fig=None):
    if codec is None:
        codec = rcParams['animation.codec']
    if bitrate is None:
```

```
        bitrate = rcParams['animation.bitrate']
    if fig is None:
        fig = plt.gcf()

    anim = SessionAnimation(fig, interval=interval, repeat=False)
    # frame rate (not interval) in seconds (not milliseconds)
    writer = SessionWriter(1000.0 / interval, codec, bitrate)

    grabby = lambda *x: writer.grab_frame()
    anim.event_source.add_callback(grabby)
    try:
        anim.save(filename, writer=writer)
        yield fig
    finally:
        writer.cleanup()
```

It makes a lot of sense to implement the session recorder as a context manager. This allows us to guarantee that the cleanup action is performed. If you have not worked with the contextmanager decorator before, it is a convenient way to create simple context managers from a function with a single yield statement in it. Everything before the yield statement is effectively part of the __enter__() portion of the context, while everything after the yield statement is effectively part of __exit__(). The value of the yield statement is the return value for __enter__().

If what was just said made absolutely no sense because you have never made a class that can be used in a with statement, then just realize that when the record_session() function is called as part of a with statement, it will do everything up to the yield statement. Then anything in the scope of the with clause is executed next. Upon leaving the scope of the with clause, the execution of the record_session() function will resume after the yield statement to wrap everything up. Context managers are extremely powerful this way because they allow you to create useful functions that can "bookend" arbitrary code. As the author of record_session(), we don't have to worry at all about what the user is doing while the yield statement is being processed because our code is completely self-contained. Prior to context managers, the solution to this problem would have been to pass an arbitrary function for record_session() to call, which gets unwieldy when users need to wrap sections of code into functions for single use purposes.

So, let's see this session recorder in action:

Source: `chp3/session_recorder.py`

```
if __name__ == '__main__':
    with record_session('session.mp4') as fig:
        ax = fig.add_subplot(1, 1, 1)
        ax.plot([1, 2, 3, 4, 5])
        plt.show()
```

The `record_session()` context manager returned a figure to use for plotting (we can only record a movie for a single figure). We can then use the figure as one normally would, performing plotting actions and ending with the usual `plt.show()` call. Go ahead and try out the example. When the figure is displayed, pan the plot around a bit, then close the figure. The encoding will then wrap up and produce a movie file. Play back this movie file and you will see the plot get panned around in exactly the same way you just did in the interactive session.

One important limitation to keep in mind when using the session recorder is that the figure should not be resized while the session is interactive. Movie formats assume a static size for its duration, so if we start sending the encoder frames that are sized differently from the first frame, the video will start to alias as the encoder blindly crams pixels into incorrectly sized boxes. At this time, Matplotlib cannot disable figure resizing to protect users from messing up their own recordings.

On a related note, it is not recommended that you supply the keyword argument bbox_inches='tight' to the `savefig_kwargs` argument in the animation's `save()` method. This argument shaves off any extraneous whitespace around the saved figure. It is an extremely popular autotrimming feature in Matplotlib. However, if even one frame is sized differently from the others by even one pixel, the video will be ruined.

Summary

We have seen how easy it is to integrate an animation into any Matplotlib application. Using `FuncAnimation`, we were able to simulate a user stepping through the frames of our application and save it as an animated GIF. Furthermore, we saw how to control the speed of the animation, whether or not the animation should loop, and if so, how much of a delay should be inserted between loops. Besides function-based animations, the `ArtistAnimation` class was introduced as a simple alternative animator, discussing the pros and cons of each. As we became more advanced in our animation usage, we were able to create and synchronize multiple animation instances, allowing developers to mix together the desired animation elements.

We also covered other advanced animation topics, such as how animation objects in Matplotlib work, in particular, the timers in the animator classes. We discussed why Matplotlib's cross-platform timer object is necessary and how it works for interactive sessions. Taking it a step further, we used timers within our interactive application without even invoking any animation code at all. Then, we discussed the blitting optimization that is available when the overhead cost of drawing the static elements of your animations in each frame approaches the time it takes to render the animated portions, and how this optimization comes with a price. Finally, we covered some advanced animation recipes to give some ideas on how to achieve some commonly requested effects, such as tails and fades.

Then we covered how the animation objects save movie files. The difference between codecs and container formats were discussed briefly. More importantly, a table was provided showing the compatibility of the different combinations of codecs and containers with various display and presentation software on different platforms. Then, we showed how to save multiple animation objects into a single movie using the `extra_anim` keyword argument. The movie writer framework was introduced, as well as an overview of the entire movie-saving process. Finally, to demonstrate how one could manipulate the pieces of this animation stack, it was shown how one could modify an existing stream writer into an interactive session recorder for Matplotlib.

In the next chapter, we will extend our application further, adding tools and other visual elements to it. It is time to add some bling to our app!

4
Widgets

What are widgets? They are doohickeys, you know, thingamajiggers or whatchamacallits. Whatever they are, they are the visual tools by which a user can interact with your application. Humans intuitively interact with their environment through physical objects. It is perfectly natural for us to want to have knobs, buttons, and other contraptions to get things done. Up to this point, most of our interactivity has been through the keyboard or using default interactivity via the mouse. We have not added any knobs or buttons to our application in order to extend its functionality.

A word of warning before we proceed. This chapter will often exhibit feature creep. This will be necessary in order to demonstrate the features that Matplotlib provides; however, it does not mean that one should pack every single possible widget into their application just because they can. Developing an application in such a manner leads to clutter. Take care to consider your requirements and how best to accomplish them.

Built-in widgets

A design principle adopted early on by Matplotlib was one of interoperability. It shouldn't matter which GUI you are using; everything should just simply work. Therefore, Matplotlib provides a basic set of widgets that are entirely implemented using Matplotlib's interactivity framework. All of the built-in widgets are implemented using nothing more than what we have covered in this book so far. While these widgets may not be the most aesthetically pleasing ones, they will work in any interactive environment that you use for regular plotting.

Conceptually, many widgets emit specialized events that can have callbacks attached by developers. However, the mechanism to attach these callbacks is much more direct than the more generalized event handling that we worked with back in *Chapter 2, Using Events and Callbacks*. This makes working with widgets accessible to inexperienced programmers who are yet to learn how to create a GUI application.

Indeed, given that the primary audience for Matplotlib is scientific programmers for whom GUIs are, at best, an afterthought, Matplotlib provides a gradual curve to create full-fledged GUI applications. For simple GUI tasks, one can go quite far with Matplotlib without ever having to adopt a GUI platform. And, as we will see in the next chapter, taking those final steps into a GUI application would not require getting rid of any existing code.

Slider

So the manager drops by your cubicle and says, "Yeah, so, here is the thing. The Bobs hate pressing buttons on the keyboard to go back and forth through the radar loop. If you could make it more like a video player with a little moving bar at the bottom, that would be great." Well, it is a good thing that Matplotlib has the Slider widget. It is very basic and simple to use. It is initialized with an Axes object and would act as a progressive bar depicting a value between some minimum and maximum value that is set upon creation. More importantly, it is designed to respond to mouse clicks anywhere within the bar, thus triggering callbacks with the new value of the bar.

For our storm cell application, we have most of the mechanisms in place for this via the custom 'frame_changed' event. To add a Slider object, we will need to allocate some space in the figure, create the object, and attach a callback that would update the display whenever the slider experiences a change. Let's first create a utility function that takes a figure object, the number of frames, and a height parameter as a fraction of the figure space. Assume that the widget module is imported from the matplotlib package in the following code snippet:

Source: chp4/slider.py

```
def build_progress_bar(fig, lastframe, height):
    # Give us some room along the bottom
    fig.subplots_adjust(bottom=2*height)
    barax = fig.add_axes([0.1, 0.005, 0.8, height])
    bar = widgets.Slider(barax, 'Time', 0, lastframe, valinit=0,
                        valfmt='%d of '+str(lastframe))
    return bar
```

Existing subplots are adjusted at the bottom to give space for twice the height requested because we need to accommodate any axes labels and tick labels. We then manually create a new `Axes` object using a method that we are yet to cover in this book. The `add_axes()` method is known as the direct axes insertion method as it bypasses much of the pyplot and figure-subplot-handling mechanisms. It is trickier to use in some respects because you are now operating outside of the figure's subplot specification mechanism, but it will do exactly as you request it and will not be impacted by anything else in the figure. The argument to `add_axes()` is a list of *x* position, *y* position, and width and height, all in "figure space", which is essentially just normalized space between 0 and 1. Keep in mind that the origin of this space is in the lower left-hand corner of the figure.

Finally, the `Slider` object is created with the `Axes` instance. It is given a label to display along with a number range of 0 to `lastframe`. We will also specify the starting point for the slider at zero. As a feature of the slider, its current value is displayed on its right. Because we are dealing with integer frame numbers, we will need to specify that the display should be formatted for integers and include a cue for how many frames there are.

Next, we will call this function from within the `ControlSys` constructor:

```
self._progress_bar = build_progress_bar(
        fig, data.shape[0] - 1, 0.02)
```

Also, we will add a callback to this slider to update the display whenever the user interacts with the slider:

```
self._progress_bar.on_changed(
        lambda frame: self.change_frame(int(frame)-self.i))
```

So, whenever the slider exhibits a change, it will call the `change_frame()` method of `ControlSys` to move back or forward a specified number of frames. Note that for the `Slider` instance, the callback will be given a single argument, which is the floating point value that the slider represents. So, we will need to cast it as an integer prior to performing the subtraction and passing it to the method that expects an integer. At this point, the application will change frames in response to both key presses and interactions with the slider. The user can click anywhere along the bar, and the display will change to the corresponding frame. Furthermore, the user can go back and forth between the two input methods, and mostly, it will work just fine.

There is one last piece that we need to put in place. As it stands, there is no way to communicate frame changes back to the slider. So, when a user uses the keyboard to advance a few frames, the slider is not updated accordingly, leading to much confusion. This has to be addressed carefully. By default, any changes to the slider's internal value will trigger an event, which would cause the change_frame() method to be called, which would then cause the 'frame_change' event to be emitted. Since we need to use this event to ensure that the slider is updated appropriately when a key is pressed, a closed cycle is formed, causing a feedback loop.

Fortunately, the solution is simple. We will connect a new callback to the 'frame_change' event:

```
self._connect('frame_change', self.update_progress_bar)
```

Then, we will define a new method for ControlSys that will carefully update the slider without triggering an event:

```
def update_progress_bar(self, index):
    self._progress_bar.eventson = False
    self._progress_bar.set_val(index)
    self._progress_bar.eventson = True
```

Just about all of the Matplotlib widgets have an attribute named eventson that is typically set to True. Emission of an event is protected by this attribute. So, if we set it to False prior to calling the progress bar's set_val() method, which would normally trigger callbacks, then the slider can do everything it needs to do to update the bar visually without triggering callbacks. We would then restore the attribute to True as we wrap up. The following figure shows the slider bar:

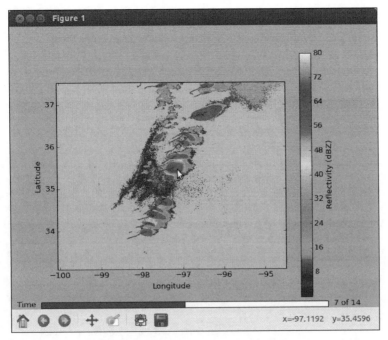

Slider bar without miniature hamburgers

Go ahead and try out the script in the *Slider* section for yourself and see how much more user-friendly the application will become with such a simple little widget.

Button

Given that the Bobs didn't like using the keyboard to go back and forth through the radar loop, most likely they don't like to use the keyboard for other things as well. I know this is utter blasphemy and completely incomprehensible to developers and power users who love their keyboard shortcuts, but some people just love having buttons on their screens with the exact name of their function written on them. I know! It is crazy, but what can you do?

The widget module of Matplotlib provides a `Button` class. Each instance is given an `Axes` object and a string for its label. You can optionally provide an image to be displayed on the button (which can be any valid argument to Matplotlib's `imshow()` function) as well as the button colors when the mouse cursor is and is not hovering over the button. The image option is very nice for those who want to make their buttons look like real GUI buttons that are prevalent in GUI applications. You load up an icon image using Matplotlib's `plt.imread()` function and provide its returned object as the image argument. For our purposes, we will stick with just having text in our buttons.

Given that we are going to want a button for just about all of our keymap items, let's implement our button system in a similar manner as our `KeymapControl` class:

Source: `chp4/buttons.py`

```
class ButtonControl:
    def __init__(self, fig, width, height):
        self.fig = fig
        # Give us some room along the top
        fig.subplots_adjust(top=1-height*2)
        self._buttonwidth = width
        self._buttonheight = height
        self._buttonmap = {}

    def connect_buttonmap(self):
        for text, (cid, func, button) in self._buttonmap.items():
            if cid is None:
                cid = button.on_clicked(func)
                self._buttonmap[text] = (cid, func, button)

    def disconnect_buttonmap(self):
        for cid, func, button in self._buttonmap.values():
            if cid is not None:
                button.disconnect(cid)
                self._buttonmap[text] = (None, func, button)

    def add_button_action(self, text, action_func):
        if not callable(action_func):
            raise ValueError("Invalid action. Button '%s''s"
                             " action is not a callable" % text)
        if text in self._buttonmap:
            raise ValueError("'%s' is already a button" % text)
        ax = self.fig.add_axes(
                (len(self._buttonmap) * self._buttonwidth,
                 0.99 - self._buttonheight,
                 self._buttonwidth, self._huttonheight))

        button = widgets.Button(ax, text)
        # Swallow the event parameter. Not needed for these buttons
        func = lambda event: action_func()
        cid = button.on_clicked(func)
        self._buttonmap[text] = (cid, func, button)
```

The constructor is rather different than the constructor of KeymapControl. We still need a dictionary that will map the label to not only the function, but also the function's callback ID and the button object itself. In this design, we are limiting ourselves to a single callback per button, but the Button widget itself does not have that restriction (indeed, none of the built-in widgets have that restriction). Also, note that to disconnect a callback function from a button you do not use the figure's canvas via the mpl_disconnect() method, rather you do it directly through the widget object instead using its disconnect() method.

The ControlSys class now subclasses ButtonControl along with the other control classes, and the constructor will build itself a set of buttons that have a width that is 10 percent of a figure and height that is 5 percent of a figure:

```
ButtonControl.__init__(self, fig, 0.1, 0.05)
```

Also, we will add some buttons through the constructor as well:

```
self.add_button_action('|<<',
                       lambda : self.change_frame(-5))
self.add_button_action('|<',
                       lambda : self.change_frame(-1))
self.add_button_action('>|',
                       lambda : self.change_frame(1))
self.add_button_action('>>|',
                       lambda : self.change_frame(5))
self.add_button_action('Del', self.delete_selected)
self.add_button_action('Save',
                       lambda : self._emit('save', None))
self.add_button_action('Help',
                       lambda : self._emit('help', None))
```

The following figure shows the output of the preceding code:

Buttons--because the keyboard and slider are just not enough

The functions and lambdas attached to these buttons are identical to the ones passed to their keymap counterparts. Try out the script in the *Button* section. You will find that you can now change the frame of the radar loop in three ways — arrow keys on the keyboard, the four buttons we just added, and the slider. Also note that changing the frame using any of the new buttons still updates the slider, but yet required no new code to do so. All the pieces came together through the event interface. Lest we forget, the changing of the frames updates multiple things, independently, that is, the radar image, the polygons, the tracks, and the slider bar. If we had a new requirement to display something else on a frame-by-frame basis, such as the timestamp of each radar image, then adding it would be a simple matter and would be inherently controllable by all of the input methods.

Check buttons

This application has three major display elements, that is, the radar image, storm polygons, and tracks. While all three should be displayed at the same time most of the time, it is entirely reasonable to want to independently hide these elements. Implementing such a feature through just the keyboard is possible but it would start to clutter up the keymap, and it would require tracking multiple states, thus cluttering up the code as well. GUI checkboxes are a useful tool to not only provide an interface for tracking multiple independent states, but also for providing a useful visual cue on the current boolean state of each item you need tracked. The Matplotlib library provides a simple CheckButtons widget for this very purpose.

The `CheckButtons` constructor takes an `Axes` object in which all of the checkboxes and text labels will reside, as well as a list of strings for the labels. There will be as many checkboxes as there are labels. Finally, the constructor takes a list of Booleans of the same length as that of the list of labels. The booleans would indicate the initial activity state of each button, `True` will have the box checked, while `False` will have an empty box.

To implement our checkboxes, we will follow a similar design pattern that we used for the slider. We will start with a utility function that will be supplied with the figure instance as well as the width of the widget. The function will adjust the subplots in the figure to make some room on the right-hand side of the figure, make the needed `Axes` object, and then build the `CheckButtons` widget:

Source: chp4/check_buttons.py

```
def build_check_buttons(fig, width):
    # Give us some room along the right
    fig.subplots_adjust(right=1-width)
    boxax = fig.add_axes([0.99 - width, 0.8, width, 0.1])
    checks = widgets.CheckButtons(boxax, ('Radar', 'Polys', 'Tracks'),
                                  [True]*3)
    return checks
```

Note that because we are placing the widget on the right-hand side of the plot, we need to adjust the figure margin by `1 - width` instead of `width`. The use of `0.99` as the offset when constructing the `Axes` object is to give a slightest bit of a gap from the edge. Our checkboxes will be labeled **Radar**, **Polys**, and **Tracks**, and will all be set as active initially. Next, we will need to call this function in the `ControlSys` constructor and attach a new method as a callback to the returned widget:

```
        self._toggle_buttons = build_check_buttons(fig, 0.1)
        self._toggle_buttons.on_clicked(self.toggle_visibility)
```

The new `toggle_visibility()` method would initially seem easy to implement. It takes a single argument, that is, the string label originally given to the `CheckButtons` constructor. This is the label for the checkbox that was changed:

```
    def toggle_visibility(self, item):
        if item == 'Radar':
            self.raddisp.im.set_visible(
                    not self.raddisp.im.get_visible())
        elif item == 'Polys':
            self.polygons.toggle_polygons(self.i)
        elif item == 'Tracks':
            self.lines.tracks.set_visible(
                    not self.lines.tracks.get_visible())
        else:
            raise ValueError("Invalid name %s for toggling" % item)
        self.fig.canvas.draw_idle()
```

However, this would not work properly for the polygons. The problem is that the storm cell polygons are represented as a list of `PolygonCollection` objects, one for each frame that individually have their visibility turned on and off. Toggling the polygons in this manner would only take effect in the current frame. This is another example of the need to keep the data separate from the display. The logical concept of the storm cell visibility as a whole does not perfectly line up with the visibility of the individual storm cells. The `Stormcells` class needs to carry a logical visibility state. Let's modify `Stormcells` to use a `_visible` attribute:

Source: `chp4/check_buttons.py`

```python
def toggle_polygons(self, frame_index, visible=None):
    if visible is None:
        visible = not self.polygons[frame_index].get_visible()
    self.polygons[frame_index].set_visible(
        visible and self._visible)

def get_visible(self):
    return self._visible

def set_visible(self, visible):
    self._visible = bool(visible)
```

So, whenever the visibility for the `Stormcells` object is `False`, no individual polygon can be made visible, even if the user calls the `toggle_polygons()` method directly. This keeps the state consistent. The final form of the `toggle_visibility()` method is as follows:

Source: `chp4/check_buttons.py`

```python
def toggle_visibility(self, item):
    if item == 'Radar':
        self.raddisp.im.set_visible(
                not self.raddisp.im.get_visible())
    elif item == 'Polys':
        self.polygons.set_visible(
                not self.polygons.get_visible())
        self.polygons.toggle_polygons(
                self.i, self.polygons.get_visible())
    elif item == 'Tracks':
        self.lines.tracks.set_visible(
                not self.lines.tracks.get_visible())
    else:
        raise ValueError("Invalid name %s for toggling" % item)
    self.fig.canvas.draw_idle()
```

The following screenshot shows the use of check buttons to choose which display element to show in our application:

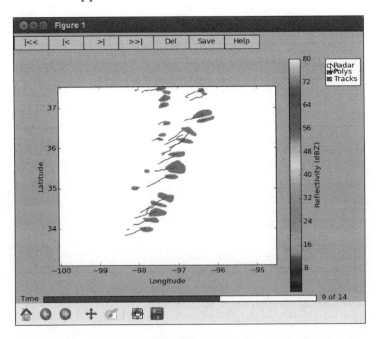

Calling the `toggle_polygons()` method after setting the visibility would ensure that the current frame's polygons are taken care of automatically. The users of our application now have the ability to choose what they want to see for their own purposes. Giving users the freedom to choose how to use your application allows it to become a more general-use tool. On the other hand, too much freedom can make an application too confusing or cluttered to use. Also, without a clear design in place, users may start requesting new features now that your application provides a hint of new possibilities. Try to strike a good balance in your designs.

Radio button

The storm cell application is becoming more and more interactive, but it is still missing some key components. Primarily, we have no way to mark any new storm cells to our dataset. Doing so will require mouse interaction, but how do we do this without conflicting with the existing polygon-picking feature? We will need to make our application modal. There needs to be two modes in which the mouse interacts with the plot — selection and outlining. These two modes can easily be chosen via key presses, but let's also add a little widget for this too. This way, our users can have an easy-to-see visual cue for the mode they are currently in, which would help to reduce user confusion and mistakes.

A widget that maintains a mutually exclusive state among multiple items is typically referred to as a set of radio buttons. The Matplotlib library has such a widget available, and we will use it for our mode-setting needs. The RadioButtons constructor is very similar to the CheckButtons constructor. It takes an Axes instance as well as a list of labels. However, instead of a list of booleans to indicate which label is active or not, the constructor takes an integer index into the supplied list to indicate which label should be initially active.

Following the same design pattern that we used for the check buttons previously, we will place this particular widget in the upper right-hand corner of the figure. We start with a utility function:

Source: chp4/radio_buttons.py

```
def build_radio_buttons(fig, height):
    # Give us some room along the top
    fig.subplots_adjust(top=1-height)
    button_ax = fig.add_axes([0.85, 1 - height, 0.14, height])
    buttons = widgets.RadioButtons(
            button_ax, ('Selection', 'Outline'))
    # Compatibility layer (this method was not added until v2.1.)
    if not hasattr(buttons, 'set_active'):
        def set_active(index):
            if 0 > index >= len(buttons.labels):
                raise ValueError("Invalid RadioButton index: %d" %
                                 index)

            for i, p in enumerate(buttons.circles):
                if i == index:
                    color = buttons.activecolor
                else:
                    color = buttons.ax.get_axis_bgcolor()
                p.set_facecolor(color)

            if buttons.drawon:
                buttons.ax.figure.canvas.draw()

            if not buttons.eventson:
                return
            for cid, func in buttons.observers.items():
                func(buttons.labels[index].get_text())
        buttons.set_active = set_active
    return buttons
```

The first few lines should be quite familiar. After that, however, it is a bit of what is called "monkey patching". Until recently, the RadioButtons widget in Matplotlib was missing a method to independently set the state of the widget without an event. We were able to do this with the Slider object earlier in this chapter, and such a feature was very important to maintain consistency between the state of the display and the application. Therefore, this utility function will monkey patch a set_active() method onto this RadioButtons instance that would set the appropriate button active and all other buttons inactive. It will also, if needed, trigger any callbacks, passing them the label of the button that was made active. This is an interesting insight into the inner workings of many of the Matplotlib widgets, as many of the widgets we have discussed so far follow this particular pattern.

Next, we will need to call this utility function from the ControlSys constructor and have it maintain a _mode attribute (initializing it to the default 'Selection' mode):

```
self._mode_buttons = build_radio_buttons(fig, 0.1)
self._mode = 'Selection'
```

Also, we will attach all of the callbacks, not only for the radio buttons, but also to add two new keys 'o' and 's' for the outline and selection modes, respectively:

```
self._mode_buttons.on_clicked(self.set_mode)
self.add_key_action('s', 'Selection mode',
                    lambda : self.set_mode('Selection'))
self.add_key_action('o', 'Outline mode',
                    lambda : self.set_mode('Outline'))
```

Of course, we will need to add a new ControlSys method to set the mode:

```
def set_mode(self, mode):
    if mode != self._mode:
        self._mode_buttons.eventson = False
        if mode == 'Selection':
            self.connect_picks()
            self._mode_buttons.set_active(0)
        elif mode == 'Outline':
            self.disconnect_picks()
            self._mode_buttons.set_active(1)
        else:
            self._mode_buttons.eventson = True
            raise ValueError("Invalid mode value: %s" % mode)
        self._mode_buttons.eventson = True
        self._mode = mode
```

This method is very important to understand. While we could have implemented the handling of the changing of mode via the same event framework we have for other things, let's keep it procedural to ease understanding. First, nothing will happen unless the mode is actually being changed. If the mode stays the same, then there is no need to do anything. Second, much like we needed to do to independently set the `Slider` widget's state earlier in the chapter, we don't want to cause a feedback loop. So, we will set the mode button's `eventson` attribute to `False`. This will prevent the triggering of callbacks when we do update the widget. Next, depending upon the mode being set, we will either connect or disconnect the picking ability of `ControlSys`, which is entirely the point of setting the mode. Next, we will call the widget's `set_active()` method with the appropriate index, which will visually update the widget to the correct state. Finally, as we exit the method, we will restore the `eventson` attribute and record the mode for the `ControlSys` class. The output of this is demonstrated in the following screenshot:

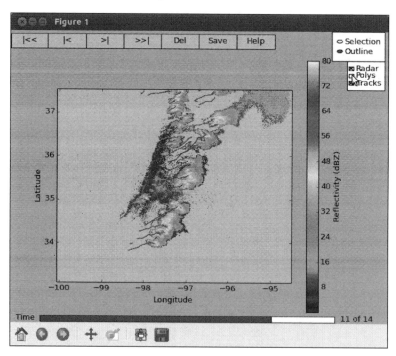

Selecting the 'Outline' mode using the radio buttons

If you run the script in this section, you will not see much difference from before. There will be a new widget in the upper right-hand corner and that's pretty much it. Now press the *o* key. You will see that the radio buttons are automatically updated to show that the mode is now set to **Outline**. Try selecting a polygon. You will find that you cannot. Now click on the **Selection** radio button and you will find that you can select a polygon again. As a side note, press the *h* key for the help menu. The menu will automatically gain two new entries for the two modes.

Lasso

It is a bit ironic that this feature is one of the last ones we will cover in this chapter, as it was this widget that I first encountered and became convinced that a full-fledged GUI application was not necessary for an early project involving storm cells. The ability to interactively draw a polygon directly upon a radar image is an absolute requirement for a storm cell editor application. Without the ability to add polygons for a new radar loop, all we have is just a radar viewer with too many widgets.

The Lasso widget in Matplotlib is a fair bit different from other widgets we have encountered so far. First, this widget does not persist; it is created on demand. Second, it is used in two parts, activation and deactivation. A lasso records the points your mouse passes over between the activation time of the widget and its deactivation. This makes it perfect for the task of obtaining storm cell outlines in our application. We will use mouse button presses and releases to signal these two stages. While it is technically possible to use a different event to trigger the start of a lasso, Matplotlib's implementation of the class is somewhat short-sighted as it assumes that the left mouse button (and only that button) is continuously held down while drawing, and it is only the release of that button that would trigger the finishing step of the lasso. Future versions of Matplotlib may generalize this somewhat to allow other mechanisms to control the lasso, such as a combination of the keyboard and mouse.

To implement the storm cell outline drawing feature, let's start with updating the ControlSys class with two new methods for the activation and deactivation of Lasso:

Source: chp4/lasso.py

```
def _start_stormcell(self, event):
    if self.fig.canvas.widgetlock.locked():
        return
    if event.inaxes is not self.raddisp.im.get_axes():
        return
    if self._mode != 'Outline':
        return
    self._lasso = widgets.Lasso(event.inaxes,
                                (event.xdata, event.ydata),
                                self._finish_stormcell)
    self.fig.canvas.widgetlock(self._lasso)

def _finish_stormcell(self, verts):
    if len(verts) > 2:
        self._emit('create', (self.i, verts))
    self.fig.canvas.widgetlock.release(self._lasso)
    self._lasso = None
    self.fig.canvas.draw_idle()
```

The _start_stormcell() method will check three things to figure out whether it should even start the process of creating a storm cell polygon. First, it checks the canvas to see whether another widget has already acquired a lock. Certain kinds of widgets inherently cannot operate concurrently, such as the panning and zoom-to-rectangle widgets. The canvas instance maintains an advisory lock mechanism that widgets can query and also acquire when it is available. For the second check, the method will check to see whether the event that triggered occurred from within the Axes instance that we want to draw in. Remember that all of the other widgets we currently have are Axes instances themselves. We do not want to use a lasso in any of those axes whenever the user clicks inside one of them. The last check is to determine whether the ControlSys instance is currently in the **Outline** mode, otherwise we wouldn't want to use a lasso.

Once the checks pass, a Lasso object is created. The Lasso constructor is supplied with the Axes instance that it will operate in, the first vertex for the polygon that it will be drawing, and the callback that it should use when the left mouse button is released. The instantiated Lasso object is saved as an attribute of the ControlSys instance. Finally, a widget lock is acquired from the canvas to prevent other widgets from interfering with the Lasso object during its lifetime.

When the release event is triggered, the `Lasso` widget provides the *x* and *y* vertexes that had been recorded in the `_finish_stormcell()` method that was set as the callback. First, you need to conduct a check to ensure that the `verts` variable contains at least three *x* and *y* tuples. This helps eliminate storm cell outlines that would occur from spurious mouse clicks. Furthermore, a polygon with less than three points has a nonexistent area, which makes it very difficult to select and delete later. If the check passes, then we will emit a `'create'` event, supplying a tuple of the frame index and the list of vertexes. As part of the finishing step, we then release the widget lock, delete the `Lasso` instance by setting the `_lasso` attribute to `None`, and trigger an idle draw (which would get rid of the lasso's outline).

If you were to run the code at this point after switching to the **Outline** mode, you will be able to use the mouse to draw a polygon anywhere you'd like on the radar image. When you release the mouse button, the outline will disappear. This is because we have yet to attach any callbacks to the emitted `'create'` event. This event is the opposite of the `'delete'` event. Currently, we have two callbacks attached to the deletion event—one to delete a particular polygon from the `Stormcells` instance and one that would delete it from the storm data held by the `ControlSys` object. Similarly, we will need to create two new methods, one in the `Stormcells` class and one in `ControlSys`, which would add a new storm cell. First, let's add the `add_polygon()` method for the `Stormcells` class:

```
def add_polygon(self, celldata):
    frame_i, verts = celldata
    paths = self.polygons[frame_i].get_paths()
    paths.append(Path(verts, closed=True))
    lws = self.polygons[frame_i].get_linewidths()
    lws.append(1)
```

This method looks much like the `delete_polygon()` method, except that we are appending a `Path` object instead of "popping" it off of the `paths` list. Similarly, for line widths, we append a value of `1` to the list. The `Path` object is a specialized Matplotlib data structure for lists of vertex data—be it a line, Bezier curve, or a polygon—and is imported from the `matplotlib.path` module. Because we are dealing with a polygon, we pass a `closed=True` argument to the constructor so that it can ensure that the path's first vertex is also the path's last vertex.

Next, we create the method used to add a new storm cell to the storm data held by
ControlSys:

Source: chp4/lasso.py

```
def add_stormcell(self, celldata):
    frame_i, verts = celldata
    stormcell_index = len(self.stormdata)
    xcent, ycent = np.mean(verts, axis=0)
    newcell = np.array([[(xcent, ycent, frame_i, np.nan,
                         calc_area(verts),
                         stormcell_index, -9,
                         np.array(verts))],
                       dtype=storm_dtype)
    self.stormdata = np.append(self.stormdata, newcell)
    self.stormmap[frame_i] = np.append(self.stormmap[frame_i],
                                       stormcell_index)
```

The add_stormcell() method demonstrates some very simple, but useful NumPy
features. First, the verts list is a list of list, which NumPy can interpret as a two-
dimensional array. To compute a rough estimate of the polygon's center coordinate,
one can call np.mean() on the vertexes, applying the mean along the zeroth
dimension. Because the list of vertexes is N rows by two columns, such a calculation
results in two values being returned. Note that this is just an approximation of the
polygon's center because the vertexes are not guaranteed to be uniformly spaced
along the outline.

Next, we create a new one-element NumPy-structured array (similar to the array that
we discussed back in the *Chapter 2, Using Events and Callbacks*). This array contains
the *x* and *y* center point, the frame index, frame time, the area of the polygon, the
storm cell's index, the storm cell's track ID number, and a NumPy array of vertexes
for the polygon. What's not shown here (but included in tutorial.py) is the calc_
area() function that can approximately calculate the area of a polygon recorded as
latitude/longitude points. For now, we will set the frame time to NaN because we
have not coded a way for ControlSys to know what time it is (as opposed to what
frame it is, which it does know). Most importantly, the track ID is set to -9 because
this is the value used elsewhere to indicate that the storm cell has not been associated
with any storm tracks.

This array is appended to the stormdata attribute, remembering that NumPy arrays
cannot change size. So, np.append() will return a new array that we will assign
back to the stormdata attribute. Finally, the stormmap list of NumPy arrays, each
containing a list of storm cell indexes, is updated with this new storm cell's index.

The only thing left to do now is attach these two methods as callbacks to the
`'create'` event:

```
self._connect('create', self.polygons.add_polygon)
self._connect('create', self.add_stormcell)
```

The following screenshot demonstrates drawing a polygon around a storm cell while
in the **Outline** mode:

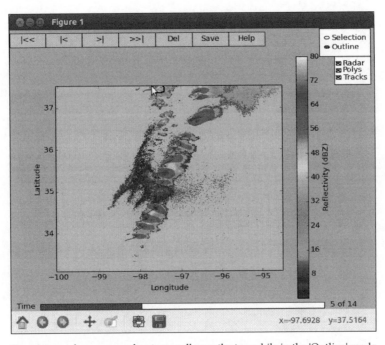

Drawing a polygon around a storm cell near the top while in the 'Outline' mode

When you run the script in this section and switch to the **Outline** mode, you will
find that any outline you draw now will persist. If you switch back to the **Selection**
mode, you can pick these polygons and delete them if you wish.

LassoSelector

This particular widget is slightly different from the `Lasso` widget (and is a somewhat
recent addition to Matplotlib). The primary difference is that this widget is persistent
as opposed to being created on demand. Because it is persistent, its usage is a bit
more simplified. The constructor only needs the `Axes` instance for which it applies
and the callback to use when a polygon selection has been made. This object will
manage the widget locks for you. The callback only needs to do something with the
list of vertexes.

For our purposes, if we were to use the `LassoSelector` widget instead of the `Lasso` widget, we would create the widget upon the switch to the **Outline** mode and destroy it when we switch away from that mode. At that point, we could eliminate the `_start_stormcell()` method and get rid of its connection to the `'button_press'` event.

RectangleSelector

You are actually already acquainted with this particular widget. It is primarily used to select a region to zoom in the built-in interface. However, it can certainly be used for other purposes as well, such as selecting multiple items within its box or just be a way to draw an arbitrary rectangle (or line) on your plot. Let's take a break from our storm cell application for a moment and come up with an example of using the `RectangleSelector` widget:

Code: `chp4/rectangle_selector.py`

```python
from __future__ import print_function
import numpy as np
import matplotlib.pyplot as plt
from matplotlib.widgets import RectangleSelector
from matplotlib.path import Path

class DataContainer(object):
    def __init__(self, xs, ys):
        self.xs = xs
        self.ys = ys

    def select_from_bbox(self, x1, y1, x2, y2):
        bbox = Path([(x1, y1), (x1, y2), (x2, y2), (x2, y1)],
                    closed=True)
        return bbox.contains_points(zip(self.xs, self.ys))

if __name__ == '__main__':
    xs, ys = np.random.random((2, 25))
    fig, ax = plt.subplots(1, 1)
    ax.scatter(xs, ys)

    def how_many_selected(evnt_click, evnt_release):
        print(evnt_click.xdata, evnt_click.ydata)
        print(evnt_release.xdata, evnt_release.ydata)
        where = how_many_selected.dc.select_from_bbox(
                    evnt_click.xdata, evnt_click.ydata,
```

```
                    evnt_release.xdata, evnt_release.ydata)
        print("%d out of %d" % (np.sum(where), len(where)))
    how_many_selected.dc = DataContainer(xs, ys)

    rs = RectangleSelector(ax, how_many_selected)
    plt.show()
```

Setting up the widget is easy. The constructor, at a minimum, needs the relevant `Axes` instance and a callback function that would be called upon the release of the relevant mouse button. Unlike most callback functions that are used for widgets, this one takes two arguments, both of which are `Event` objects representing the event that started the selection and the event that ended the selection. More often than not, one would only be interested in their `xdata` and `ydata` attributes, but all the other attributes that we discussed for mouse events back in *Chapter 2, Using Events and Callbacks*, are available as well.

The following screenshot shows the use of `RectangleSelector` in the box mode to select points:

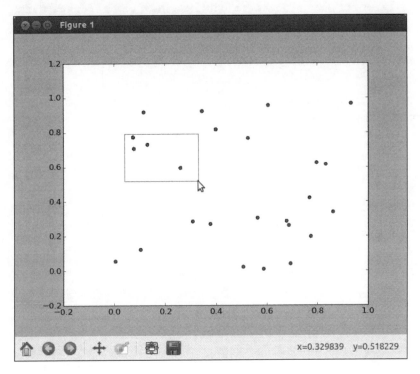

There are many other arguments that can be added to the constructor. To avoid triggering a selection action inadvertently, there are `minspanx` and `minspany`, which set the minimum thresholds in the respective dimensions. There is also `drawtype`, which can be set to either `'box'`, which is the default, or `'line'`. With the widget set to a line-drawing mode instead of a box mode, one can easily turn the widget into a ruler:

Code: `chp4/ruler.py`

```python
from __future__ import print_function
import numpy as np
import matplotlib.pyplot as plt
from matplotlib.widgets import RectangleSelector
from mpl_toolkits.basemap import Basemap, pyproj


def distance(evnt_click, evnt_release):
    g = pyproj.Geod(ellps='WGS84')
    _, _, dist = g.inv(evnt_click.xdata, evnt_click.ydata,
                       evnt_release.xdata, evnt_release.ydata)
    print("(%f, %f) to (%f, %f): %f km" %
            (evnt_click.xdata, evnt_click.ydata,
             evnt_release.xdata, evnt_release.ydata,
             dist / 1000.0))


if __name__ == '__main__':
    fig, ax = plt.subplots(1, 1)
    bm = Basemap(projection='cyl', resolution='l',
                 llcrnrlon=-130, llcrnrlat=25,
                 urcrnrlon=-60, urcrnrlat=55)
    bm.drawstates(ax=ax)
    bm.drawcountries(ax=ax)
    bm.drawcoastlines(ax=ax)
    rs = RectangleSelector(ax, distance, drawtype='line',
                           minspanx=0.001, minspany=0.001)
    plt.show()
```

Run the script in this section and you will see a map of the USA. Click anywhere on the map and drag. You will see a straight line connected to your mouse pointer from the initial click point. Release the mouse button and information will be printed to your terminal, indicating the longitudes and latitudes of the start and end points as well as the great circle distance between them. Because the `RectangleSelector` widget is set up to be persistent, you can measure distances as many times as you like. This prevents the zoom tool from working because it is also a `RectangleSelector` widget; however, you can still zoom using the scroll button of your mouse. Also note that you can still pan the plot as you could before, as shown next:

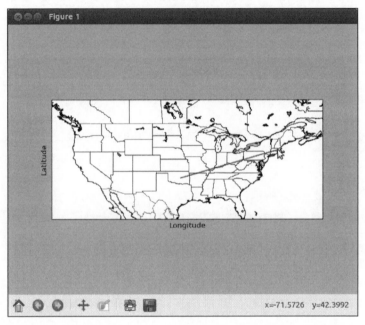

Using the RectangleSelector in its 'line' draw type to measure the distance from Oklahoma to Massachusetts (~2,333 km)

Slated for version 2.1 of Matplotlib is an overhaul of the toolbar system to make it possible to extend its default set of tools. Essentially, it will become possible for developers to register and unregister the individual tools that you find in the toolbar and other tools that you make or are provided by third-party packages. With this feature, the ruler tool would automatically switch off whenever the zoom tool is chosen, preventing conflicts, and there would even be a button in the toolbar for the widget, if you so choose.

SpanSelector

The SpanSelector widget is much like the RectangleSelector widget, except that it is adjustable only in a single dimension. This particular widget can be useful to highlight regions in a plot, or for easy calculations of aggregate statistics or integrations over a particular dimension, or for easy zooming in or out of a region without modifying the limits of any other dimensions. It mostly works in a similar manner, too. Its constructor expects an Axes instance to attach the widget to, and it expects a callback function for when the selection is complete. Unlike the callback method for RectangleSelector, which took two Event arguments, this callback takes two arguments that are the start and end values of the selected span, rather than the start and end Event instances. Let's take a look at an example that creates different colored highlights for a time series of fake stock prices:

Code: chp4/span_selector.py

```python
from itertools import cycle
import matplotlib.pyplot as plt
from matplotlib.widgets import SpanSelector
import numpy as np

if __name__ == '__main__':
    t = np.arange(180)
    value = (20 * np.sin((np.pi/2) * (t / 22.0)) +
             25 * np.random.random((len(t),)) + 50)
    fig, ax = plt.subplots(1, 1, figsize=(10, 5))
    ax.step(t, value)
    ax.set_ylabel("Stock Price (USD)")
    ax.set_xlabel("Time (days)")
    colors = cycle(list('rybmc'))

    def onselect(x0, x1):
        ax.axvspan(x0, x1, facecolor=next(colors), alpha=0.5)
        fig.canvas.draw_idle()

    ss = SpanSelector(ax, onselect, 'horizontal')
    plt.show()
```

In addition to the `Axes` instance and the callback function, `SpanSelector` needs to know its orientation. It can be either `'horizontal'` or `'vertical'`. In the preceding example, once a selection is made, that region remains highlighted, but with a different color that comes from the cyclic iterator of colors. Like `RectangleSelector`, this widget can also have its properties defined through the `rectprops` argument and can also have a `minspan` attribute defined to provide a basic filter of selections. Besides the `minspan` attribute, one can temporarily disable the widget by setting its visibility to `False` and re-enable it by making it visible again. The following screenshot shows selecting spans of data in a time series:

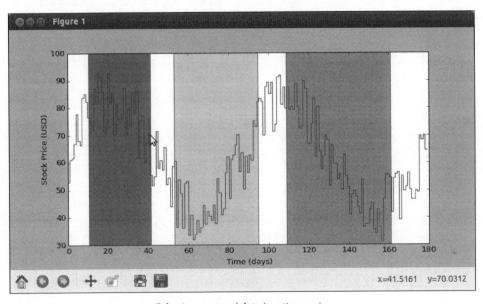

Selecting spans of data in a time series

One feature of `SpanSelector` that does not currently exist in `RectangleSelector` is that one could provide another callback method for any mouse movement events during the selection via the `onmove_callback` argument. This callback gets the same set of arguments as the selection callback. As of version 1.4, one can also specify that the rectangle should remain after the selection is complete by setting `span_stays` to `True`. The selection remains visible until the next selection is made. Note that for our example, we did not use the `span_stays` argument. Instead, we plotted an `axvspan()` upon selection.

Cursor

This particular widget does not add any interactive features like the others do with callbacks and such, but it is a simple display widget that can add just the right touch to their interactive application. Invoke this widget for an `Axes` object. Whenever the mouse goes over the plot region, a horizontal and vertical line will appear, intersecting at the mouse pointer, following it around. If you only want the vertical line, then set `horizOn=False` in the constructor. Set `vertOn=False` if you want only the horizontal line instead. Note that you can also set these two properties of the `Cursor` instance after the fact and turn it all off with the `visible` property. Any additional keyword arguments to the constructor can specify the properties of the lines such as `color` and `linewidth`.

format_coord()

This isn't a widget in the same manner as the others that we have discussed here. Rather, it is a hook into a built-in interactive feature of `Axes` objects. All `Axes` objects have a `format_coord()` method that is called whenever the mouse moves over the plot area. This method returns a string that is displayed in the lower right-hand corner of the figure. By default, they display the x and y data coordinates of the mouse pointer. This is straightforward enough because the method takes two arguments, that is, the x and y coordinates of the mouse in data space (therefore, the values would always be within the x and y limits of the plot). However, there is no reason why it can't display something else as a function of those coordinates.

There are a couple of different ways in which one could modify this method. The easiest way (but a little hackish) is to monkey patch the `format_coord()` method with a customized function. One could also subclass `Axes`. The following example uses the subclassing approach to display not only the x and y coordinates, but also the image value if there is an image:

Source: `chp4/format_coord_image.py`

```python
import numpy as np
import matplotlib.pyplot as plt
from matplotlib.axes import Axes
import matplotlib.transforms as mtransforms
import matplotlib.projections as mproj

class DataAxes(Axes):
    name = 'data'
    def format_coord(self, x, y):
        normal_part = Axes.format_coord(self, x, y)
        if self.images:
```

```
        # Most recent image is usually on top
        im = self.images[-1]
        j, i = self._coords2index(im, x, y)
        z = im.get_array()[j, i]
        return "Value: %f, %s" % (z, normal_part)
    return normal_part


@staticmethod
def _coords2index(im, x, y):
    """
    Convert data coordinates to index coordinates.
    Credit: mpldatacursor developers.
    Copyright (c) 2012. BSD License
    Modified from original found at:
    https://github.com/joferkington/mpldatacursor/blob/master/
mpldatacursor/pick_info.py
    """
    xmin, xmax, ymin, ymax = im.get_extent()
    if im.origin == 'upper':
        ymin, ymax = ymax, ymin
    im_shape = im.get_array().shape[:2]
    data_extent = mtransforms.Bbox([[ymin, xmin],
                                    [ymax, xmax]])
    array_extent = mtransforms.Bbox([[0, 0], im_shape])
    trans = (mtransforms.BboxTransformFrom(data_extent) +
             mtransforms.BboxTransformTo(array_extent))
    j, i = trans.transform_point([y, x]).astype(int)
    # Clip the coordinates to the array bounds.
    return (min(max(j, 0), im_shape[0] - 1),
            min(max(i, 0), im_shape[1] - 1))


# Register DataAxes so that it can be used like any other Axes
# Uses the 'name' attribute, so it will be accessible as 'data'.
mproj.projection_registry.register(DataAxes)
```

This is fairly straightforward, even if it may seem a bit obtuse at first. The `DataAxes` subclass defines two methods, the modified `format_coord()` method and a helper method, namely, `_coords2index()`. In `format_coord()`, we first obtain what would normally be the output for a typical `Axes` instance. Then, we determine whether the instance has had any image objects plotted onto it (the `self.images` attribute is a list of image objects as `imshow()` can be called multiple times over different extents).

For simplicity, we will assume that the last image added is at the top above all others and that that image is the one we want to reference. Ideally, we would have a list of image objects sorted by their zorder value in descending order. We would then— again, ideally—march through that list, looking for the first image object that has the *x* and *y* coordinates within its extents. For the purposes of this example though, we will ignore all other possible image objects.

Next, because our coordinates are in data space, we will need to transform these coordinates into integer array indexes with all the proper bound clipping as well. This is done using Matplotlib's built-in transform system. Again, for simplicity, we will assume that only linear scales are at work (for example, not using scales such as log, semilog, or polar transformations). To build this linear transform, we construct two bounding boxes as mtransforms.Bbox instances and create a transform object, which can then be used to calculate the array coordinates. Because the mouse could potentially be off the image object but still within the plot region (for example, after panning the plot or zooming out), we will need to clip the array coordinate values to be within the array bounds. So, when the mouse is off the image, the array indexes returned by this method will be the point on the edge of the image closest to the mouse pointer.

Finally, we register the DataAxes class so that it can be used much like any other built-in Axes objects. This is done through Matplotlib's projection system. The original intent of this registration system was to have an Axes subclass for each kind of projection, such as polar projections and 3D projections, but it is perfectly legitimate to use this registration system for specialty Axes classes. Now that the DataAxes class has been registered, it is easy to request it:

Source: chp4/format_coord_image.py

```
if __name__ == '__main__':
    ys, xs = np.mgrid[0:5:0.1, 0:4:0.1]
    fig = plt.figure()
    ax = fig.add_subplot(1, 1, 1, projection='data')
    ax.imshow(xs, extent=(xs[0, 0], xs[0, -1], ys[0, 0], ys[-1, 0]),
              origin='lower', cmap='gray')
    plt.show()
```

The projection='data' argument to fig.add_suplot() tells Matplotlib to use whichever Axes class that was registered as data. For the plt.subplots() function, this can be specified by providing a single element dictionary, {'projection':'data'}, to the subplot_kw argument.

The following screenshot displays the image value under the mouse cursor with our
`DataAxes` subclass:

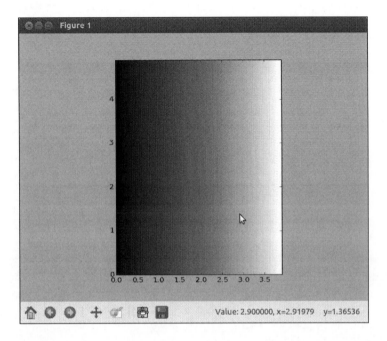

Run this script and move your mouse cursor over the image. You will see the image
value reported along with the coordinates in the lower right-hand corner of the
figure window. Pan and zoom the figure and it will still work exactly as expected.

Third-party tools

While Matplotlib likes to follow a "batteries included" philosophy for all things
related to plotting, there are times when a desired feature just doesn't generalize
well enough for it to be a standard feature. Alternatively, a feature may require other
specialty packages that do not make sense to have as a dependency for Matplotlib.
For these situations, there is a growing library of packages that provide additional
interactive features on top of your standard Matplotlib application.

mpldatacursor

The **mpldatacursor** package (https://pypi.python.org/pypi/mpldatacursor) provides a number of useful interactive tools, primarily focusing on making it very easy to annotate a plot. To use this tool, create your plots as normal. Then you can add a data cursor to one or more `Axes` object (and can optionally specify which `Artist` objects the cursor is valid for). Then, click on something in your plot and an annotation will appear, describing what you clicked on.

Glue

The Glue project (http://www.glueviz.org) is not a widget or a tool, but it builds entirely off of Matplotlib to provide the means to interactively explore high dimensional datasets, particularly relational data. Once a dataset is loaded up in Glue, one can tell it to create different kinds of plots such as histograms and images. Interacting with one plot would automatically update other plots that are related to the one you interacted with. For example, one could select a region of the histogram, and the data points that fall within that selected region would get highlighted in the corresponding image plot. Conversely, one could also select a region from the plot display, and the histogram display would be updated with a histogram overlay of the selected region. New plots can also be generated from arbitrary slices of existing images (for example, a 2D slice through a 3D "cube" of data). There are also other useful widgets to make data exploration easy and intuitive.

Plot.ly, ggplot, prettyplotlib, and Seaborn

The Plot.ly, ggplot, prettyplotlib, and Seaborn projects are also not widgets, but they are very useful projects that builds off of Matplotlib. Plot.ly (http://plot.ly) is a plotting web service that can take a Matplotlib figure and host an interactive version of it on its web servers. You can then share that plot with others to interact with and modify. Finally, you can export that figure back to Matplotlib code or several other languages, such as R or Matlab, with support for more languages in the works. The ggplot project (https://github.com/yhat/ggplot) is a Python clone of the popular R package by the same name. It is a high-level way of creating plots using a concept called "Grammar of Graphics".

The prettyplotlib project (http://blog.olgabotvinnik.com/prettyplotlib/) and the Seaborn project (http://web.stanford.edu/~mwaskom/software/seaborn/) both do a fantastic job of not only improving upon the default aesthetics of Matplotlib, but also making it very painless to modify these settings both programmatically and interactively. The Seaborn project in particular also provides additional interactive tools for statistical analyses.

Summary

Interactivity takes many forms. Widgets are visible elements that are primarily interacted with via the mouse. In this chapter, we covered all of Matplotlib's GUI-neutral widgets. Widgets such as sliders, checkboxes, and radio buttons were all integrated into our application's event framework. Doing so allowed for multiple ways to update the state of the application and for the state of the widgets to be updated as well. Widgets such as `Lasso` and `Button` were added as input mechanisms, providing the means to modify the data that the application displays. Other widgets were also covered but not included into our main application such as `RectangleSelector` and `SpanSelector`. A few ways of using these widgets were demonstrated, from selecting data to measuring distances. We even went over how to create a specialized `Axes` subclass that operates seamlessly with the rest of Matplotlib for the purpose of extending the data display of the figure window.

Finally, we went over a variety of third-party tools and packages, some providing widgets, some providing an alternative interface to Matplotlib and everything in between. If these projects do not provide what you need, create your own package to grow this community. Hopefully, this chapter has provided insight into Matplotlib's flexibility and has inspired new widgets and features, some of which we may find in a future version of Matplotlib!

In the next chapter, we will dive just a little bit deeper into Matplotlib. Its GUI neutrality will be violated. We will pull back that canvas and begin to explore Matplotlib's deepest secrets.

5

Embedding Matplotlib

The Lion thought it might be as well to frighten the Wizard, so he gave a large,
loud roar, which was so fierce and dreadful that Toto jumped away from him in
alarm and tipped over the screen that stood in a corner. As it fell with a crash
they looked that way, and the next moment all of them were filled with wonder.
For they saw, standing in just the spot the screen had hidden, a little old man,
with a bald head and a wrinkled face, who seemed to be as much surprised as
they were. The Tin Woodman, raising his axe, rushed toward the little man
and cried out, "Who are you?"

"I am Oz, the Great and Terrible," said the little man, in a trembling voice.

- The Wonderful Wizard of Oz, by L. Frank Baum

We now have a working, usable, interactive application that demonstrates many features of Matplotlib. Let us take a quick look back at what we have. First and foremost, we have a way to display images with additional plotting on top of it. We can pan and zoom that figure, and resize it to our heart's content. Next, the application responds to custom key mapped commands that we added for this specific application. We also added other features such as object selection via the mouse. Our application now also utilizes timers to produce timed effects such as transitions.

Those features are all well and good, but it was in the previous chapter where our interactive application became something more recognizable by everyday users. The addition of GUI widgets to our application makes it somewhat more intuitive to use and more adaptable to different workflow habits. Users now have multiple ways to interact with the application and can use the method that best suites them for maximum productivity. All of this was achieved without needing to know how to use any GUI toolkits.

There is a trade-off, however. The GUI-neutral widgets that Matplotlib provides are not aesthetically pleasing, to say the least. Nor are they very customizable. They can also be very difficult to manage in a larger, dynamic application with many moving parts. The requirements for your application can easily grow beyond what Matplotlib can provide you.

Your manager drops by your cubicle. "So... yeah... I just gave your storm application a try, and I think it is broken. Uhm, the menu bar seems to be missing along the top, you see? If you can get right on that, that would be great, mmm-kay?"

Well, we could kludge together a bunch of `Text` objects in an `OffsetBox`...ahh, but we wouldn't be able to always put it at the very top, and it would be fragile anyway. So, is this the point where we part ways? Was this entire venture all for naught? Were the Matplotlib developers so shortsighted as to have us completely stymied by a mere menu?

No! Of course not! Why would you think such silly thoughts?

Think back to the very beginning of the first chapter: "Matplotlib's philosophy is to give the developer full control, but without being stupidly unhelpful and tedious." You may have not noticed, but this entire book has been an exercise in progressively taking control from Matplotlib as we developed our application. Never once did we feel truly hemmed in by it. So, what trick do I have up my sleeve to get us out of this predicament? No tricks. Just a thought for you: "Don't those buttons for the navigation toolbar look remarkably polished compared to the buttons we placed within our application?"

While you ponder that thought, let us look at our problem a different way. Consider a situation where an existing GUI application gains a requirement for interactive plotting. For example, a spreadsheet-like application that now needs to be able to plot the data dynamically, with zooming and panning. Much time and resources have been spent developing this application, so it doesn't make sense to scrap it. Nor do we want to spend the time coming up with a limited plotting module that will just become a maintenance nightmare. If only you could use an existing plotting package right inside your application.

The revelation

You have had a moment to ponder the question about the toolbar buttons. Some of you may have even gone back to the application, and ran it using different backends, realizing that all the toolbars follow their respective backend's style. That would mean that it is somehow possible to include GUI-specific elements into our Matplotlib application. Or perhaps it is the Matplotlib figure that is the odd one out, with it being included into a tiny GUI application that is the backend?

Indeed, this whole time, you have been embedding Matplotlib figures into a GUI!

Everything in Matplotlib builds off the figure's canvas object. That canvas is the interface layer between the user and the backends. By staying above this layer, most of the messy details about GUI applications have been tucked away, keeping the user focused on their plotting tasks. Matplotlib's appeal is in giving the user a plot in as little as three lines of code: the import, the plot, and the show. Not once does the user need to give a thought to initializing an application object, attaching a figure window to it, then drawing the plot, and then finally triggering the GUI `mainloop`.

Once you go beyond the canvas layer, you are locking your application into a specific GUI toolkit. The trade-off being that you can access the full suite of features provided by your toolkit of choice. In this chapter, we will examine this from two perspectives: how to embed GUI elements into an existing Matplotlib application, and how to embed the Matplotlib canvas into an existing GUI application. But first, let us get to understand the Matplotlib figure better.

Through a glass, darkly

Previously in this book, we have conflated the canvas and figure terms, at best giving an impression that the figure object was merely a container for the canvas object. When working above the canvas level, this conceptual model is sufficient. The truth, however, is more complicated. There are actually three objects in play: figure, canvas, and manager. We encountered the manager briefly in one of the examples in the previous chapter. While I would love to describe a very clean and inspired design involving these three objects, that would not be possible. Abstraction layers that hide away messy details are never simple. Initial appearances can often be misleading in understanding the relationships between them. Our discussion of the design should bring about a new level of clarity in how Matplotlib truly works, and hopefully some inspiration in new ways to use the library.

Tinker tailor soldier pylab_setup()

In this book, we have shown an attribute hierarchy of `figure.canvas.manager`, implying that the manager is a child object of the canvas, and a grandchild of the figure object. That would be a useless simplification. These objects all cross-reference each other in such ways that the usual parent/child object relationship has very little meaning.

There is a very good reason why nearly every Matplotlib example you find imports `matplotlib.pyplot` (either directly or through `pylab`). The import of `pyplot` triggers a call to `matplotlib.backends.pylab_setup()`, which loads the desired backend module, the `new_figure_manager()` function, the `draw_if_interactive()` function and the backend's `show()`. The backend's `show()` and `draw_if_interactive()` functions take the appropriate steps for their respective backends to display and update a figure window. This is why `matplotlib.use()` has to be called prior to the import of `pyplot` (either directly or indirectly). The import of `pyplot` can only ever happen once, so `pylab_setup()` would only be called once (actually, that is a bald-faced lie, but we won't get into the particulars about `pyplot.switch_backend()`).

The `new_figure_manager()` function is only ever called from `plt.figure()`. Its job is to instantiate an appropriate `Figure`, `FigureCanvas`, and `FigureManager` objects, and return the manager instance. Initialization of the manager requires a canvas object, which, in turn, requires a figure. This is the source of the implied hierarchy, but each object has references to each other, for the most part.

The job of the manager is to be responsible for the three high-level GUI elements in a figure: window, canvas, and the navigation toolbar. For example, if a user specifies that the figure should change size, then the manager would interpret that as a request to change the window size as well. Creation of the manager automatically creates a main window object and a navigation toolbar object and packs the supplied canvas object with the toolbar into the window.

The figure object, as we discussed in *Chapter 1, Introducing Interactive Plotting*, is an `Artist` object in its own right. It exists primarily as the root node for the hierarchy of `Artist` plotting objects and for holding a few convenience methods. It may be useful to think of the figure as the application window that contains the canvas, but it is really the canvas that contains the figure, and the application window contains the canvas.

It is important to recognize that the manager is not strictly required for use of the figure or canvas. The existence of the manager is the key distinction between simply augmenting your Matplotlib application with GUI elements and fully embedding the canvas into your own GUI application. The manager subsumes many of the tedious and oftentimes boilerplate tasks for creating and destroying the GUI window and kicking off the `mainloop`. It will be shown later in this chapter how to completely cut out the manager in order to embed your plot into your own application.

Canvas materials

Each backend subclasses `FigureCanvasBase` to create its own powerful canvas class. Because the canvas object is intended to be an interactive component in its own right, the interactive backends will typically subclass not only `FigureCanvasBase`, but also a relevant widget class from their toolkit.

These parent GUI classes of the canvases are all abstract container types. Therefore, they can have other widgets added to them as well as be able to be packed into a window such as Qt's `MainWindow` object with other widgets. The manager object does just this, packing the canvas with a navigation toolbar. The navigation toolbar also subclasses a relevant widget class from the respective toolkit.

All figure managers have at least three attributes: `canvas`, `toolbar`, and `window`. It only references the figure object through the `canvas` attribute. The following table lists what those respective instances subclass.

Backend	canvas	toolbar	window
Gtk | Gtkagg | Gtk3agg | GtkCairo | Gtk3Cairo	`gtk.DrawingArea`	`gtk.Toolbar`	`gtk.Window`
Macosx | CocoaAgg	`NSView | NSImageView`	`NSObject | (no toolbar)`	`NSWindow`
Qt4 | Qt4agg	`QtGui.QWidget`	`QtGui.QToolBar`	`QtGui.QMainWindow`
Qt5 | Qt5agg	`QtWidgets.QWidget`	`QtWidgets.QToolBar`	`QtWidgets.QMainWindow`
Tkagg | Windowing	`tk.Canvas*`	`tk.Frame`	`tk.Tk`
Wx | Wxagg	`wx.Panel`	`wx.ToolBar`	`wx.Frame`

[* Not subclassed directly. Instead, it keeps a `tk.Canvas` instance accessible via `get_tk_widget()`.]

Understanding exactly what the canvas and other parts are made of will greatly ease the embedding process. Some backends' managers may have additional attributes to assist with the GUI layout process. We will go over some of these differences in the next section on embedding GUI elements into an existing Matplotlib application.

Bars, menus, and sliders – four ways

Perhaps the best way to really understand the roles of these objects is through examples. Let us look at two simple tasks for modifying our storm cell application: add a menu bar and replace the Matplotlib slider widget with a similar native widget. We will do this same thing using four different GUI toolkits: GTK, Tkinter/Tcl, wxWidgets, and Qt.

A word of warning before we proceed: I am, by no means, an expert in any of these GUI toolkits. Describing me as a novice would be a stretch as well. The following examples are not intended to illustrate best practices in using the toolkits. Instead, they are intended to help inspire the readers to see the possibilities and to help get one over some of the initial hurdles that one may encounter.

Another quick note regarding our storm track application. The `Tracks`, `RadarDisplay`, and `Stormcells` classes have been moved out of the application into submodules; we will no longer be needing to modify these classes any further.

GTK

The GTK library is very popular among Linux developers, but it also works on Windows and Mac systems. Most Linux systems will already have this package and its Python bindings installed, and binary installs for this toolkit for Windows and Mac are available as well. Unfortunately, most of the popular Python distributions such as Anaconda do not make GTK available and the binary installs of GTK do not easily work with those distributions. For such distributions, the toolkit needs to be built from source against the Python distribution. None of these issues, however, specifically relates to Matplotlib. Once GTK and its Python bindings are installed and working, Matplotlib can use its `gtkagg` backend right away. Matplotlib also supports other GTK-related backends such as GDK and a combination of GTK and Cairo graphics.

The following example will use the GTKv2-based backend because I have some experience with its API. The GTKv2 API does not support Python 3, though. To use GTK in your Python 3 application, you would need to use GTKv3 with **gobject introspection** through the `gtk3agg` backend, which also works in Python 2.x. As with the other backend examples, we will show that once you have locked yourself into a particular backend, you will need to explicitly set that backend prior to any other Matplotlib import.

Source: `chp5/slider_gtk.py`

```
from __future__ import print_function
import matplotlib
matplotlib.use('gtkagg')
from collections import OrderedDict
import numpy as np
import matplotlib.pyplot as plt
from scipy.io import netcdf_file
from matplotlib import widgets
from tutorial import storm_loader, storm_saver, storm_dtype, calc_area
from elements import RadarDisplay, Stormcells, Tracks


import gtk
```

Import of the GTK toolkit is very straightforward and simple. For the progress bar, we will redo the `build_progress_bar()` function to construct a `gtk.HScale` object. In GTK, this class is similar to the scrollbars, but it is also used for these sorts of sliders.

```
def build_progress_bar(fig, lastframe, height):
    # An abstract object that represents a set of possible values
    # on a number line, and how to move along that line.
    # Constructor takes:
    # value, lower, upper, step-increment, page-increment, page-size
    adj = gtk.Adjustment(0, 0, lastframe, 1, 5, 0)

    # The slider object
    bar = gtk.HScale(adj)
    bar.set_digits(0)  # We have integers, so show no decimal places
    bar.set_value_pos(gtk.POS_RIGHT)
    bar.show()

    vbox = fig.canvas.manager.vbox
    # Put the slider at the bottom of the packing
    vbox.pack_end(bar, expand=False, fill=False, padding=0)
    return bar
```

GTK, like some other toolkits, uses layout objects. The GTK backend has a `gtk.VBox` object into which the canvas and the navigation toolbar have been packed into it. The canvas was first packed to the start of the vertical layout box, while the navigation toolbar was first packed in to the end of the box. Therefore, when it comes to packing the slider, it will be placed above the navigation toolbar. We are going to forgo setting any heights for the slider as that can be tricky to do properly in GTK's layout system. We will see examples of how to do this in other backends, though.

We will need to change the setting of the progress bar's callback upon changes to the slider. More specifically, for GTK, the changes to the slider's stored `Adjustment` object represent the slider's state. The value of this object is accessible via the `value` attribute. Let us modify the original _progress_bar.on_changed() method call to the following:

```
self._progress_bar.get_adjustment().connect('value_changed',
        lambda adj: self.change_frame(int(adj.value) - self.i))
```

Finally, for the progress bar, we will need to modify the `update_progress_bar()` method so that the slider will respond to the `'frame_changed'` event. Again, the `Adjustment` object is obtained, and its value is set. This does not trigger a `'value_changed'` event. Therefore, we do not need to set any `eventson` attributes the way we needed to for Matplotlib's slider widget.

```
def update_progress_bar(self, index):
    self._progress_bar.get_adjustment().value = index
```

Next, we will add a very simple menu bar to our application. We will follow the same style as the code for our slider widget, creating a builder function that will be called by our `ControlSys` constructor. It will take a figure object and a dictionary of actions. We will expect four named actions: `'save'`, `'exit'`, `'help'`, and `'about'`.

```
def build_menubar(fig, actions):
    # File menu items
    save = gtk.MenuItem("Save")
    save.connect('activate', actions['save'])
    exit = gtk.MenuItem("Exit")
    exit.connect('activate', actions['exit'])
```

```
filemenu = gtk.Menu()
filemenu.append(save)
filemenu.append(exit)

# The File menubar item
filem = gtk.MenuItem("File")
filem.set_submenu(filemenu)

# The Help menu items
helpi = gtk.MenuItem("Help")
helpi.connect('activate', actions['help'])
about = gtk.MenuItem("About")
about.connect('activate', actions['about'])

helpmenu = gtk.Menu()
helpmenu.append(helpi)
helpmenu.append(about)

# The Help menubar item
helpm = gtk.MenuItem("Help")
helpm.set_submenu(helpmenu)

# Now adding File and Help menus to the bar
mb = gtk.MenuBar()
mb.append(filem)
mb.append(helpm)
mb.show_all()

vbox = fig.canvas.manager.vbox
vbox.pack_start(mb, expand=False, fill=False, padding=0)
# Put this menubar at the top by putting it first in the
# packing list
vbox.reorder_child(mb, 0)

return mb
```

Like with the slider bar, we will need the manager's vbox object again. This time, we will want the menu bar to appear at the top above the canvas, which has already been packed. So, we go ahead and pack it normally, and then call vbox.reorder_child() to move it to index 0 of the packing list. Some Linux users (depending on the desktop environment) may not see a menu bar in the figure window. Rather, it will show up at the top of the screen where most menu bars appear for native apps of those environments.

```
menuactions = {'save': lambda _: self._emit('save', None),
               'exit': gtk.main_quit,
               'help': lambda _: self._emit('help', None),
               'about': lambda _: self._emit('about', None)}
self._mbar = build_menubar(fig, menuactions)
```

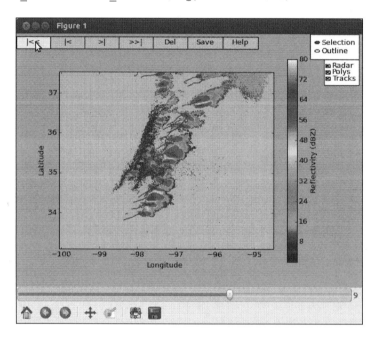

Embedding GTK's slider widget. Notice that the menu is not visible in the application window because native GTK applications of my desktop environment have their menus in a separate menu bar.

The menu items that we created were connected to an 'activate' GTK event, with an attached callback. The dictionary above provides those callbacks and most of them should be familiar. For GTK, these callbacks would be called with an argument, which we will swallow for most of them. The new callback here for 'exit' is how one would terminate GTK's mainloop. Note that this would close out all figure windows, not just the ControlSys's figure window.

Tkinter

The Tk/Tcl GUI toolkit won't be winning any beauty contests any time soon, but it has a distinct advantage of being included by default in every Python install. This greatly simplifies the installation procedure for your application. Do note that when building Matplotlib from source, you will need the Tk/Tcl development header files available in order for the Matplotlib build process to compile the tkagg backend. This often causes confusion among first-time developers because installing the Tk/Tcl header files after building Matplotlib will not make the tkagg backend be available. The Matplotlib library would have to be re-built once the header files are available. However, binary installs of Matplotlib, whether from Python wheels, Anaconda, binstar.org, or some other distribution, will have the tkagg backend already compiled and available to use.

Source: chp5/slider_tk.py

```
from __future__ import print_function
import matplotlib
matplotlib.use('tkagg')
from collections import OrderedDict
import numpy as np
import matplotlib.pyplot as plt
from scipy.io import netcdf_file
from matplotlib import widgets
from tutorial import storm_loader, storm_saver, storm_dtype, calc_area
from elements import RadarDisplay, Stormcells, Tracks

try:
    import Tkinter as tk  # for pre-py3k
except ImportError:
    import tkinter as tk  # for py3k
```

The try/except logic above addresses a change in naming conventions for the Tkinter package between the Python 2.x series and Python 3.x (py3k). This will help your script to be compatible with both versions of Python from a single codebase.

For replacing Matplotlib's slider, we will use the tk.Scale class. First, the object needs to know who its parent will be. This is mostly for processing events for children of widgets that are currently in focus. In this case, it makes sense to make the slider a child of the figure window, which we obtain from the figure manager. We also tell the Scale object that it will be modifying an integer variable by supplying a tk.IntVar instance. This makes sense because our slider is being used for control of discrete frames. We then specify the range for the Scale.

The `tk.Scale` class can take length and width arguments in units of pixels. This is different from the units that were needed for the Matplotlib slider widget, which expected fractions of the figure. Luckily, this is straightforward to convert. There is an attribute to all `Figure` objects called `bbox`, which represents the bounding box for the figure. It has a number of useful properties that return information about the bounding box. The `width` and `height` properties return the figure's dimensions in units of pixels. Multiplying that by the fractional height parameter would get the desired height of the scale bar.

```
def build_progress_bar(fig, lastframe, height):
    root = fig.canvas.manager.window

    length = int(fig.bbox.width)
    width = int(fig.bbox.height * height)
    bar = tk.Scale(master=root,
                variable=tk.IntVar(), from_=0, to=lastframe,
                label='Time', orient=tk.HORIZONTAL,
                length=length, width=width, showvalue=True)
    bar.pack(after=fig.canvas.get_tk_widget())
    return bar
```

Finally, we need to place the scale bar in the right location. Similar to GTK, the Tkinter toolkit utilizes a somewhat simplified packing paradigm. We do not need to explicitly create layout boxes. The `pack()` method of every widget specifies how it should be laid out in relation to other objects. In this case, we want the scale widget to be placed below the canvas widget. So, we call the `pack()` method with the canvas object as the `after` argument. Notice that the `tkagg` backend is unusual in that the canvas itself is not subclassed from a GUI widget. Instead, the widget instance is managed internally and is accessible via the canvas's `get_tk_widget()` method, so we pass that to the `pack()` method call.

In Tkinter, widget resources are set through the `configure()` method with keyword arguments. So, to set a callback function for slider interactions, we would set the `command` resource with the same callback lambda we set before for the Matplotlib slider in what was originally the `_progress_bar.on_changed()` method call. The value passed to the callback from this event is the value of the slider.

```
self._progress_bar.configure(
    command=lambda frame: self.change_frame(int(frame)-self.i))
```

Finally, to make sure that `'frame_change'` events in our application updates the slider widget, we will need to tweak the `update_progress_bar()` method. Instead of `set_val()`, it is just `set()`. Also, like in the GTK example, the event handling in Tk prevents recursive event calling, so we can remove the setting of the `eventson` attribute.

```
def update_progress_bar(self, index):
    self._progress_bar.set(index)
```

Next, we will add a menu bar to our application. The function will take a figure object and a dictionary of callbacks, much like how we did in the GTK example. In Tk, menus are rather simple. Conceptually, menus are just a list of items. These items can be additional menus that cascade from the item or commands attached to the item. Every menu item has a label, which is the displayed text.

```
def build_menubar(fig, actions):
    root = fig.canvas.manager.window
    # Creating the menubar
    mb = tk.Menu(root)

    # File menu items
    filemenu = tk.Menu(mb, tearoff=0)
    filemenu.add_command(label="Save", command=actions['save'])
    filemenu.add_command(label="Exit", command=actions['exit'])
    # Adding File to the menubar
    mb.add_cascade(label="File", menu=filemenu)

    # Help menu items
    helpmenu = tk.Menu(mb, tearoff=0)
    helpmenu.add_command(label="Help", command=actions['help'])
    helpmenu.add_command(label="About", command=actions['about'])
    # Adding Help to the menubar
    mb.add_cascade(label="Help", menu=helpmenu)

    # Display menubar and items
    root.config(menu=mb)

    return mb
```

With the completed menu bar above, it is added to the figure window as a menu. Therefore, it does not need to be added to any layout boxes or packing lists. Next, let us take a look at the callbacks that we will set for the menu commands. Callbacks for menu commands do not take any arguments, unlike for GTK. We also see how to quit a Tk window, reaching all the way down to the `quit()` method of the managed window object.

```
menuactions = {'save': lambda : self._emit('save', None),
               'exit': self.fig.canvas.manager.window.quit,
               'help': lambda : self._emit('help', None),
               'about': lambda : self._emit('about', None)}
self._mbar = build_menubar(fig, menuactions)
```

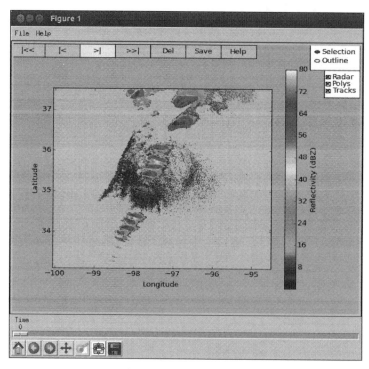

Using Tkinter's slider and menu widgets

That method should only take effect for the window and should only terminate the Tk `mainloop` once all of the figure windows are closed. All of the other callbacks are the typical callbacks we have seen before. Using this application, you will notice that the window is taller than before. This is because the canvas no longer needs to share space with the slider widget. Also, the menu bar added some height to the window.

wxWidgets

The wxWidgets toolkit is a Python-friendly library that can be a prettier alternative to Tkinter. It does need to be separately installed, thereby complicating installation procedures somewhat. However, unlike with the `tkagg` backend, the `wxagg` backend is available as soon as the wxWidgets toolkit is installed, even if it is installed after the Matplotlib package. This is because the `wxagg` backend has no compiled component. Up to version 1.4 of Matplotlib, the wxWidgets backends will not work in Python 3. At the time of this writing, the developers of wxWidgets were in the process of preparing a new release called wxPython-Phoenix that will work in Python 3. A patch for the wxWidgets backends to use the Phoenix library is slated for inclusion in Matplotlib version 2.1. Imports of wxWidgets are also the same regardless of which version of Python is being used.

Source: `chp5/slider_wx.py`

```
from __future__ import print_function
import matplotlib
matplotlib.use('wxagg')
from collections import OrderedDict
import numpy as np
import matplotlib.pyplot as plt
from scipy.io import netcdf_file
from matplotlib import widgets
from tutorial import storm_loader, storm_saver, storm_dtype, calc_area
from elements import RadarDisplay, Stormcells, Tracks


import wx
```

For the slider replacement, we can use the `wx.Slider` class. This class is similar to Tkinter's `Scale` class. It will need the window object as its parent, and the range of values. It also needs the starting value for the slider, which we will set to `zero`. One can also specify an ID number for the widget, which has uses within the wxWidgets framework that won't be covered here. This number can be safely set to `-1`. The widget's size is handled through a tuple of length and height in units of pixels. If one of the dimensions is -1, then that tells wxWidgets to automatically expand the widget in that dimension.

```
def build_progress_bar(fig, lastframe, height):
    root = fig.canvas.manager.window
    # arguments are: parent, id, startvalue, minvalue, maxvalue
    bar = wx.Slider(root, -1, 0, 0, lastframe, style=wx.SL_HORIZONTAL,
                    size=(-1, int(fig.bbox.height * height)))
```

```
sizer = root.GetSizer()
sizer.Insert(1, bar, 0, wx.EXPAND)
return bar
```

The wxWidgets framework uses `sizer` objects for layouts, similar to GTK's `VBox` and `HBox` objects. We can retrieve the window's `sizer` instance and manually insert the bar object into its packing list. Prior to this insertion, the `sizer` object for a Matplotlib figure has only two widgets packed: the canvas and the navigation toolbar. The `Insert()` method call says to insert the bar object at index 1 in the packing list, which effectively puts it after the canvas. The third argument flags how the proportions for the widget's containment area are handled. Zero for this argument indicates that there are no proportion rules to enforce onto the containment area. If a value of 1 is passed to this argument, it will equally share the vertical space with other widgets in the sizer. The fourth argument flags how the widget should be sized in relation to the parent widget. The `wx.EXPAND` flag indicates that the widget should be expanded to occupy the available space, even when the window is resized. The online wxWidgets documentation explains these parameters in far more detail than can be covered here.

Now, we need to get slider events to trigger our `'frame_changed'` event. Connecting events in wxWidgets is done through the `Bind()` method. The `Slider` class, like other widgets in wxWidgets, has many events that it can emit, giving the developer very fine-grained control over the behavior of their widgets. However, for our purposes, we only need the very general `wx.EVT_SCROLL` event, which represents any change to the slider by any means. The attached callback is passed an object from which an event object can be retrieved. From the event emitted from the slider, one can retrieve the slider's new value via the `GetValue()` method. Otherwise, the lambda callback is structured the same as it was originally.

```
cback = lambda e: self.change_frame(
        int(e.GetEventObject().GetValue()) - self.i)
self._progress_bar.Bind(wx.EVT_SCROLL, cback)
```

Finally, we need to set the state of the slider whenever the `'frame_changed'` event is emitted. Tweak the `update_progress_bar()` method to call `SetValue()` instead of `set_val()` on this slider. Setting the slider's value does not trigger an `EVT_SCROLL` event, so we don't have to worry about any protection from recursive event calling.

```
def update_progress_bar(self, index):
    self._progress_bar.SetValue(index)
    self.fig.canvas.draw()
```

Unfortunately, the `wxagg` backend is somewhat finicky. It tends to be a bit conservative in refreshing the canvas, particularly for `draw_idle()` calls. Sometimes, it needs an explicit `draw()` call. Testing of this application revealed that interacting directly with the slider would sometimes fail to update the radar display until the mouse passed over the display area, although it would work fine when using the keyboard. Adding the `draw()` method call does the trick here.

Making nice looking menus in wxWidgets is easy. First, we create a `wx.Menu` instance, and `Append()` items to it. `Append()` is a factory method that takes a specialized wxWidgets ID and a label. The wxWidgets ID in this situation can be used to tag a menu item as one of several common menu items that have default settings for them such as hotkeys. For example, marking a menu item as `wx.ID_SAVE` will cause that menu item to be accessible via the *Ctrl + S* key combination managed through wxWidgets. A value of `-1` is also appropriate as well. After creating a menu item, we `Bind()` the appropriate callback function to the `wx.EVT_MENU` signal that is emitted by it.

```
def build_menubar(fig, actions):
    root = fig.canvas.manager.window

    # File menu items
    filemenu = wx.Menu()
    fitem = filemenu.Append(wx.ID_SAVE, "Save")
    root.Bind(wx.EVT_MENU, actions['save'], fitem)
    fitem = filemenu.Append(wx.ID_EXIT, "Quit")
    root.Bind(wx.EVT_MENU, actions['exit'], fitem)

    # The Help menu items
    helpmenu = wx.Menu()
    hitem = helpmenu.Append(wx.ID_HELP, "Help")
    root.Bind(wx.EVT_MENU, actions['help'], hitem)
    hitem = helpmenu.Append(wx.ID_ABOUT, "About")
    root.Bind(wx.EVT_MENU, actions['about'], hitem)

    # Now adding File and Help menus to the bar
    mb = wx.MenuBar()
    mb.Append(filemenu, "File")
    mb.Append(helpmenu, "Help")
    root.SetMenuBar(mb)

    return mb
```

After creating the menus and binding callbacks to the menu items, we create a `wx.MenuBar` instance and append the two `wx.Menu` objects we created to it, with the appropriate labels. Finally, it is set as the figure window's menu bar, thereby avoiding the need for any `sizer` objects. Because wxWidgets wraps the GTK library on Linux, some Linux users will find that the menu bar will not appear with the figure window. As with GTK, it will be located in the desktop menu bar like any other native application in certain desktop environments.

```
menuactions = {
    'save': lambda _: self._emit('save', None),
    'exit': lambda _: self.fig.canvas.manager.window.Close(),
    'help': lambda _: self._emit('help', None),
    'about': lambda _: self._emit('about', None) }
self._mbar = build_menubar(fig, menuactions)
```

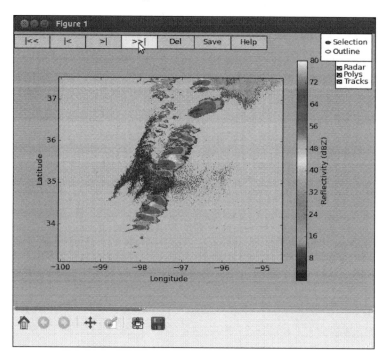

Native wxWidget slider in our application. The menu bar is separate in this screenshot due to my desktop environment.

Callbacks in wxWidgets are expected to take a positional argument, which we don't need to pass on to our menu actions. So, we will swallow them in the lambdas. We also see that a call to the `Close()` method will close a wxWidgets window. Once all of the windows are closed, the `mainloop` will terminate.

Qt

The Qt library is more than just a GUI toolkit. It is a well-designed software development platform in general. Its history, however, is quite complicated and can be very confusing for newcomers. The important thing to remember is that there is the main Qt library implemented in C/C++ and then there are the bindings for multiple languages, particularly Python. Due to a variety of reasons, there are two common Python bindings: PyQt and PySide. Matplotlib supports both bindings. Furthermore, there are multiple versions of the bindings. Starting with version 1.0, Matplotlib supported PyQt4. With **version** 1.1, support for PySide began. Then in version 1.4, support for PyQt5 was added.

Source: chp5/slider_qt4.py

```python
from __future__ import print_function
import matplotlib
matplotlib.use('Qt4Agg')
from collections import OrderedDict
import numpy as np
import matplotlib.pyplot as plt
from scipy.io import netcdf_file
from matplotlib import widgets
from tutorial import storm_loader, storm_saver, storm_dtype, calc_area
from elements import RadarDisplay, Stormcells, Tracks


from matplotlib.backends.qt4_compat import QtCore, QtGui
```

Matplotlib has various mechanisms for letting the user specify which binding to use automatically. For the developer, this means that it is best to import the Qt packages via Matplotlib's qt_compat module. This module will select the correct bindings to import automatically. It also helps to smooth out the differences between PyQt4, PyQt5, and PySide, such as PyQt5's splitting of the QtGui module into QtGui and QtWidgets. Note that qt_compat was added in version 1.4 of Matplotlib. Since version 1.1, there has been a module called qt4_compat, which is now deprecated. The qt4_compat module helps developers target the PyQt4 platform, while qt_compat lets developers target PyQt5 and later, regardless of which actual bindings are used. The examples here will use the qt4_compat module, as it is available in older versions of Matplotlib.

One difference between the Qt backends and other backends is that the navigation toolbar is at the top of the window by default. It is also detachable, meaning that the user can move it to any other position in the figure window as desired. Also, the window object is not quite like the windows in the other backends. It does not contain the navigation toolbar and the canvas widgets in a packing list. Instead, it has the canvas as a **central widget** and treats the navigation toolbar specially, which allows it to be detachable.

In the Qt library, as in GTK, layout boxes are used for sizing and placements, but the Qt backends in Matplotlib do not have any layout boxes already set. As the central widget, we will need to instantiate a `QtWidgets.QVBoxLayout` object and set it to the canvas. When we are done with building the slider and any other widgets, we can add them to the canvas's layout. But, before adding the slider, we will need to add a `QtGui.QSpacerItem` instance that, when placed before the slider in a vertical layout, will force the slider to the bottom part of the canvas.

```python
def build_progress_bar(fig, lastframe, height):
    vbox = QtWidgets.QVBoxLayout()
    fig.canvas.setLayout(vbox)
    height = int(fig.bbox.height * height)

    bar = QtGui.QSlider(QtCore.Qt.Horizontal)
    bar.setRange(0, lastframe)
    bar.setSingleStep(1)
    bar.setMinimumSize(0, height)

    # Add an auto-updating label for the slider
    value = QtWidgets.QLabel('0 of %d' % lastframe)
    value.setMinimumSize(0, height)
    value.connect(bar, QtCore.SIGNAL('valueChanged(int)'),
                lambda frame: value.setText("%d of %d" %
                                            (frame, lastframe)))

    hbox = QtWidgets.QHBoxLayout()
    hbox.addWidget(bar)
    hbox.addWidget(value)

    # This spacer will force the slider to the bottom of the canvas
    vspace = QtGui.QSpacerItem(0, 0,
            QtWidgets.QSizePolicy.Expanding,
            QtWidgets.QSizePolicy.Expanding)

    vbox.addItem(vspace)
    vbox.addLayout(hbox)
    return bar
```

As for the slider, we will use the `QtWidgets.QSlider` class, which is simple to instantiate needing only a style flag to indicate whether it is horizontal or vertical. We have to separately set this slider's range and its step size. We will go an extra step in this example and also provide a text display for the slider's current value like what was provided for with the Matplotlib slider. This requires a `QtWidgets.QLabel` instance, connected to a `valueChanged` signal emitted from the bar object. These two objects are positioned next to each other by packing them into a `QtWidgets.QHBoxLayout` instance.

We already showed how to connect to a slider event when we set up a label object to show the current frame index. We also need to trigger the `'changed_frame'` event in our application whenever the slider value changed. This will be very similar to what we did previously. We will connect the canvas (rather than the label object) to the `valueChanged` signal from the slider. The lambda callback is the same as usual because the signal provides the integer value from the slider.

```
self.fig.canvas.connect(self._progress_bar,
    QtCore.SIGNAL('valueChanged(int)'),
    lambda frame: self.change_frame(int(frame) - self.i))
```

And hooking our `'frame_changed'` event to update the slider is simple as well, requiring only a call to the `setValue()` method instead of `set_val()`. Qt is also designed, like the other toolkits, to prevent recursive event calling, so we can remove that protection here as well.

```
def update_progress_bar(self, index):
    self._progress_bar.setValue(index)
```

Finally, we will build the menu for our application. Menu items in Qt are `QtGui.QAction` instances. These constructors can take a label name and a parent widget. It can also take a `QtGui.QIcon` instance as the first argument in a three-argument form of the constructor, if you want to provide icons for your menu items. Next, you connect the menu item to the callback.

```
def build_menubar(fig, actions):
    root = fig.canvas.manager.window

    # File menu items
    saveact = QtGui.QAction("Save", root)
    saveact.triggered.connect(actions['save'])
```

```
exitact = QtGui.QAction("Exit", root)
exitact.triggered.connect(actions['exit'])

# Help menu items
helpact = QtGui.QAction("Help", root)
helpact.triggered.connect(actions['help'])
aboutact = QtGui.QAction("About", root)
aboutact.triggered.connect(actions['about'])

# Menubar creation
mb = root.menuBar()
# The File menubar item
filemenu = mb.addMenu("File")
filemenu.addAction(saveact)
filemenu.addAction(exitact)
# The Help menubar item
helpmenu = mb.addMenu("Help")
helpmenu.addAction(helpact)
helpmenu.addAction(aboutact)

return mb
```

Once all of the menu items are created, we can start adding them to the window's menu bar (obtained via the window's `menuBar()` factory method). The `addMenu()` factory method returns a `QMenu` instance with the given label set for it. The menu items are added through their `addAction()` method.

```
menuactions = {'save': lambda : self._emit('save', None),
               'exit': QtGui.qApp.quit,
               'help': lambda : self._emit('help', None),
               'about': lambda : self._emit('about', None)}
self._mbar = build_menubar(fig, menuactions)
```

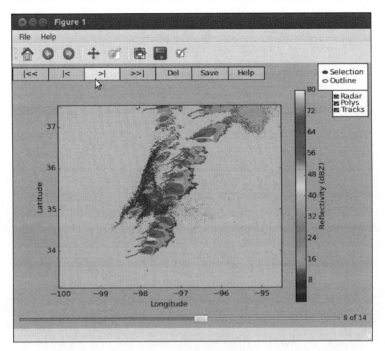

PyQt4 slider and menu bar. The slider shares space with the canvas.

Callback functions for the QAction instances are not given an argument, so the lambda functions are much like most of the other examples. This 'exit' action will quit the entire application rather than just closing out the current window. Using this version of the application, you may notice that the slider is closer to the plot area than in the other three versions, much like when we used Matplotlib's slider widget in *Chapter 4*, *Widgets*. This is because the Qt backend did not establish a layout object as the central widget. With the canvas already established as the central widget, the only solution is to pack other widgets *into* it, rather than *with* it.

Matplotlib in your app

We have peered behind the canvas and have gained an immense understanding of how backends in Matplotlib operate. For four of the major backends, we have even seen how to augment our application with GUI widgets, learning some of the subtle differences in the backends.

But, what if you already have a GUI application written in Python, and the Matplotlib portion is the new feature to add? This is called **embedding**. The basic idea is that the canvas is added to your application as a widget. The tricky part is that you cannot let `pyplot` create the `Figure` instance. The `pyplot` module assumes that it will be responsible for triggering and terminating the application `mainloop`. It also automatically attaches the figure managers to the canvases. This can conflict with normal application operations. Therefore, when embedding, it is best to completely bypass `pyplot`.

Like in the previous section, we will examine how to embed the Matplotlib canvas into a GUI Python application in four different toolkits. The application is just a main window into which the canvas is added, but you will see the minimum needed to get your Matplotlib application embedded. All of the examples will be based on the same version of the code that the previous section's examples were based on. These examples will not be built on top of those in the previous section, though. The main reason for this is that those examples would need to be reworked to remove the dependency upon the manager object. Bypassing `pyplot` means that no manager is created for the figure and canvas. It would be too confusing in this book to fix up those changes and show how to embed. Instead, we will only need to make two tiny changes in the codebase before proceeding with the embedding work—remove the following lines:

```
fig.canvas.mpl_disconnect(fig.canvas.manager.key_press_handler_id)

import matplotlib.pyplot as plt
```

The first one is of no consequence. The default keymap is established by the figure manager, and without a manager, there is no default keymap to disable! The removal of the other line keeps us from the temptation of using `pyplot`. Now, let us look at how to add our application as if it was a widget.

GTK

When skipping the import of `pyplot`, you will need to explicitly import the `Figure` class as well as the desired backend's canvas class. Of course, you will also want to import the toolkit of choice using the same approaches we used in the previous section.

Source: `chp5/embedding_gtk.py`

```
import gtk
from matplotlib.figure import Figure
from matplotlib.backends.backend_gtkagg import FigureCanvasGTKAgg
FigureCanvas = FigureCanvasGTKAgg
```

You may notice many online examples of embedding that might directly import a class called `FigureCanvas`. This is actually identical to the import of `FigureCanvasGTKAgg` from the `gtkagg` backend. As of version 1.4 of Matplotlib, the backend-specific classes for the canvas and the manager have an alias to the names `FigureCanvas` and `FigureManager`, respectively. For these examples, we will do the aliasing ourselves in order to be compatible with earlier versions of Matplotlib.

Next, we will need to see how we bypass `pyplot` to create the figure and embed its canvas into our application. For GTK, we start with a `gtk.Window` instance. Then we create a `Figure` and `FigureCanvas` objects. Notice that these are just simple calls to their constructors. After that, we are able to create plotting axes right off of the `Figure` instance like normal. That is because the only thing different at this point is the lack of the manager, and the manager wouldn't come into play in normal circumstances until the `show()`.

```
if __name__ == '__main__':
    ncf = netcdf_file('KTLX_20100510_22Z.nc')
    data = ncf.variables['Reflectivity']
    lats = ncf.variables['lat']
    lons = ncf.variables['lon']
    stormcells = storm_loader('polygons.shp')

    win = gtk.Window()

    fig = Figure()
    canvas = FigureCanvas(fig)
    ax = fig.add_subplot(1, 1, 1)
    raddisp = RadarDisplay(ax, lats, lons)
    raddisp.update_display(data[0])
    fig.colorbar(raddisp.im)
    polycolls = Stormcells(ax, stormcells)
    linecoll = Tracks(ax)

    # Turn on the first frame's polygons
    polycolls.toggle_polygons(0, True)
    ax.autoscale(True)
```

```
ctrl_sys = ControlSys(fig, raddisp, data, polycolls, linecoll,
                       stormcells)

win.connect('destroy', lambda x: gtk.main_quit())
win.set_default_size(int(fig.bbox.width), int(fig.bbox.height))
win.set_title("Embedding with GTK")
win.add(canvas)
win.show_all()
gtk.main()
```

The final block of code does much of what a manager would do normally. These steps establish the size of the main window, its title, and the adding of the canvas widget. Finally, it kicks off the GUI `mainloop`, at which point you would see the main window with your fully functioning application.

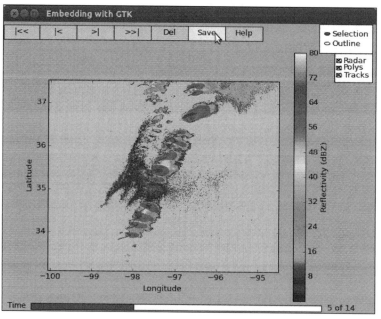

Embedding the canvas in a simple GTK application. This will appear the same in all of our embedding examples.

Yes, it was that easy. "Perhaps it was because the GUI app we were embedding into was too simple," you think? Nope. The canvas is a widget, and so it can be used in all of the same ways that GTK widgets can be used. You can add the widget just about anywhere. In a tab, in a modal window, in whatever you'd like it to be. You can also add as many canvas widgets as you'd like. Just remember that there is one canvas to each figure instance (and vice versa), but there is no reason why one can't have multiple canvas widgets to an application window.

One thing is missing from our figure, though—the navigation toolbar. This is another thing that the figure manager would take care of automatically. If you want the toolbar as well, it is available as a widget from the backend. There are examples in Matplotlib's online documentation showing how to include the toolbar. For simplicity, we will omit the navigation toolbar from these examples.

Tkinter

There is nothing unusual about the imports when embedding into a Tkinter application. You may have noticed by now the lack of the `matplotlib.use()` call. The `use()` feature is almost exclusively for the convenience of `pyplot` and is completely useless in embedding situations.

Source: chp5/embedding_tk.py

```
try:
    import Tkinter as tk
except ImportError:
    import tkinter as tk
from matplotlib.figure import Figure
from matplotlib.backends.backend_tkagg import FigureCanvasTkAgg
FigureCanvas = FigureCanvasTkAgg
```

For the Tk application, we will create a `tk.Tk` instance and pass it as the master widget for the `FigureCanvas`. The canvas classes from the different backends all have slightly different constructors, depending on the design of the toolkit and the backend.

```
if __name__ == '__main__':
    ncf = netcdf_file('KTLX_20100510_22Z.nc')
    data = ncf.variables['Reflectivity']
    lats = ncf.variables['lat']
    lons = ncf.variables['lon']
    stormcells = storm_loader('polygons.shp')

    win = tk.Tk()

    fig = Figure()
    canvas = FigureCanvas(fig, master=win)
    ax = fig.add_subplot(1, 1, 1)
    raddisp = RadarDisplay(ax, lats, lons)
    raddisp.update_display(data[0])
    fig.colorbar(raddisp.im)
    polycolls = Stormcells(ax, stormcells)
    linecoll = Tracks(ax)
```

```
# Turn on the first frame's polygons
polycolls.toggle_polygons(0, True)
ax.autoscale(True)

ctrl_sys = ControlSys(fig, raddisp, data, polycolls, linecoll,
                      stormcells)

win.wm_title("Embedding with Tk")
canvas.get_tk_widget().pack(side=tk.TOP, fill=tk.BOTH, expand=1)
canvas.show()
tk.mainloop()
```

The last block of code here sets the window title and packs the canvas widget into its parent (which is the window instance, in this case, that was specified back in the canvas constructor). Remember that the `tkagg` backend is a little bit unusual in that the canvas object itself is not the widget. Instead, you obtain the widget from a call to the `get_tk_widget()` method. Finally, the `mainloop` is started, at which point the window will appear with a fully operational Matplotlib application.

Still don't believe me that it is this easy? Take a look at the next example.

wxWidgets

Just like the previous example's imports, there is nothing special here.

Source: chp5/embedding_wx.py

```
import wx
from matplotlib.figure import Figure
from matplotlib.backends.backend_wxagg import FigureCanvasWxAgg
FigureCanvas = FigureCanvasWxAgg
```

wxWidgets is a little bit different from the GTK and Tkinter toolkits. wxWidgets has an `App` instance that needs to be constructed which will control the GUI `mainloop`. For wxWidgets, it doesn't really matter when you instantiate it, but for the sake of consistency, let us instantiate it before any of the other GUI elements. wxWidgets is also a little bit different with respect to its window constructors. The `wx.Frame` constructor requires a parent widget (which is `None` if it is the main window), an ID number (which we can safely set to `-1`), and the window title. The `wxagg` backend's `FigureCanvasWxAgg` constructor is also different from the other backend's canvas constructors. It needs the parent widget, which we are setting to the window, the ID number, and the figure instance to which the canvas will be attached.

```
if __name__ == '__main__':
    ncf = netcdf_file('KTLX_20100510_22Z.nc')
    data = ncf.variables['Reflectivity']
    lats = ncf.variables['lat']
    lons = ncf.variables['lon']
    stormcells = storm_loader('polygons.shp')

    app = wx.App()
    win = wx.Frame(None, -1, "Embedding with wxWidgets")

    fig = Figure()
    canvas = FigureCanvas(win, -1, fig)
    ax = fig.add_subplot(1, 1, 1)
    raddisp = RadarDisplay(ax, lats, lons)
    raddisp.update_display(data[0])
    fig.colorbar(raddisp.im)
    polycolls = Stormcells(ax, stormcells)
    linecoll = Tracks(ax)

    # Turn on the first frame's polygons
    polycolls.toggle_polygons(0, True)
    ax.autoscale(True)

    ctrl_sys = ControlSys(fig, raddisp, data, polycolls, linecoll,
                          stormcells)

    win.SetInitialSize(wx.Size(int(fig.bbox.width),
                               int(fig.bbox.height)))
    sizer = wx.BoxSizer(wx.VERTICAL)
    sizer.Add(canvas, 1, wx.TOP | wx.LEFT | wx.EXPAND)
    win.SetSizer(sizer)
    win.Fit()
    canvas.SetFocus()
    win.Show()
    app.MainLoop()
```

Building our wxWidgets app is a little bit different from the first two examples we looked at. I have had good success with embedding the canvas widget into a `wx.BoxSizer` instance that is then added to the `Frame` instance. Then, the window's `Fit()` method that will keep the canvas and the window sized together is called. Obviously, your application may have different needs, so choose accordingly. Also notice the call to the canvas's `SetFocus()` method. This helps to get our key press events recognized by Matplotlib right away. Finally, the `mainloop` in the app object is triggered.

And you still don't believe me that it is this easy to embed Matplotlib into your application?

Qt

One thing different for this toolkit's import is that we will need the `sys` module as well. Otherwise, it is still recommended that you import the Qt bindings through Matplotlib's `qt_compat` or the `qt4_compat` module.

Source: `chp5/embedding_qt4.py`

```
import sys
from matplotlib.backends.qt4_compat import QtGui, QtCore
from matplotlib.figure import Figure
from matplotlib.backends.backend_qt4agg import FigureCanvasQt4Agg
FigureCanvas = FigureCanvasQt4Agg
```

Like wxWidgets, the Qt toolkit also has an application object that is needed to be instantiated. However, it has been my experience that it is critical that the `QtGui.QApplication` object is created prior to any other GUI element, unlike with wxWidgets. The application constructor takes `sys.argv`, which is the list of command-line arguments. This is a common convention in Qt programming, and there are a number of Qt-specific command-line arguments that could be passed to your application for special GUI behavior, which are explained in the Qt documentation online. Next, the main window, figure and canvas objects are created.

```
if __name__ == '__main__':
    ncf = netcdf_file('KTLX_20100510_22Z.nc')
    data = ncf.variables['Reflectivity']
    lats = ncf.variables['lat']
    lons = ncf.variables['lon']
    stormcells = storm_loader('polygons.shp')

    # Must come before any Qt widgets are made
    app = QtGui.QApplication(sys.argv)
    win = QtGui.QMainWindow()

    fig = Figure()
    canvas = FigureCanvas(fig)
    ax = fig.add_subplot(1, 1, 1)
    raddisp = RadarDisplay(ax, lats, lons)
    raddisp.update_display(data[0])
    fig.colorbar(raddisp.im)
    polycolls = Stormcells(ax, stormcells)
    linecoll = Tracks(ax)

    # Turn on the first frame's polygons
    polycolls.toggle_polygons(0, True)
    ax.autoscale(True)
```

```
ctrl_sys = ControlSys(fig, raddisp, data, polycolls, linecoll,
                      stormcells)

win.resize(int(fig.bbox.width), int(fig.bbox.height))
win.setWindowTitle("Embedding with Qt")
# Needed for keyboard events
canvas.setFocusPolicy(QtCore.Qt.StrongFocus)
canvas.setFocus()
win.setCentralWidget(canvas)
win.show()
sys.exit(app.exec_())
```

Finally, with the app-building code block, we size the window and establish its title. We also take a couple extra steps to get the keypress events to be recognized by setting a `StrongFocus` policy for the canvas widget, and setting it to have the focus. Then we add the canvas as the central widget. We could have added the canvas to a tab in a tabbed window setup, or maybe as some sort of element in a dashboard display, and set that display as the central widget instead of the canvas. In such cases, the focus policy may need to be tweaked a bit to allow other widgets in the app to respond to interaction events. At last, the window is shown, and the `mainloop` is started. Qt will even determine a return value for your application based on how it terminates.

Summary

We have now seen Matplotlib for what it truly is: a plotting library that provides several miniature GUI applications. We have revealed an interloper to the figure-canvas relationship; namely the manager. The miniature GUI application provides the manager, navigation toolbar, and the GUI window in which to marry all of these components together into the interactive Matplotlib figure that we have come to depend upon. When Matplotlib is not interactive enough for you, you saw how to add new widgets to spice up your application. Finally, for those who already have an interactive application, and only need Matplotlib "on the side," we explained how Matplotlib's canvas could be treated just like another widget to be added to your application.

Looking back over the book, we have been on a journey discovering Matplotlib's interactive features. Building this application piece-by-piece has given us a valuable opportunity to not just learn the features, but to also see how they can work together to create something that is greater than the sum of its parts. For example, not only did we learn about Matplotlib's events and how to use them, we also utilized custom events to completely refactor our application. That refactoring made it possible to easily add new features to our event-driven application.

We also saw first-hand the reasons for maintaining the separation between the display and our data. Conflating the two is a common pitfall in application development; its problems often manifesting later in development when they are much more difficult to fix. With isolated display elements and the event framework, each part could operate independently of each other, which made it easy to add new elements to our display. It also made it trivial to reuse those components in completely new applications.

The Bobs were wowed by our boardroom-pleasing animations that we were able to generate from our codebase. We were also able to incorporate other animation aspects into our application such as transitions using timers, as well as learn how to create effects like tails and fades. Next, knobs and other gizmos were added to it so that users like your manager and the Bobs could feel much more comfortable using our application. Those widgets were an important component to achieving full interactivity.

No project is ever really finished. More can always be done to extend it, making it more useful. This storm cell application is an open source project hosted at my GitHub page, and is actively used for severe weather research. Patches are always welcome, and perhaps you may find a feature of yours demonstrated in a future edition of this book!

Index

F

fades 72, 73
figure
  about 9
  canvassing 10-13
file formats 75
format_coord() method 110-113
frontend
  to backend 7

G

gallery 6
ggplot
  URL 114
Glue project
  about 114
  URL 114
GTK
  about 122-126, 140, 142
  gobject introspection 123

I

IdleEvent event 24
ImageMagick tool 56
interactive backend
  versus non-interactive backend 7
interactive navigation
  about 3
  Home, Back, and Forward button 3
  Pan (and zoom) button 4
  Save button 4
  Subplot configuration button 4
  Zoom-to-rectangle button 4
interactive plotting 4

K

KeyEvent event 24
keymapping 34-38

L

LassoSelector widget 103, 104
Lasso widget 99-103
LocationEvent event 24

M

Matplotlib
  built-in keymap 32-34
  embedding 117-119
  figure-artist hierarchy 9
  forums 6
  gallery 6
  help 6
  in app 140
  installing 1, 2
  interactive backend, versus non-interactive
    backend 7
  mailing lists 6
  work, displaying 3
menus 122
MouseEvent event 24
mpldatacursor package
  about 114
  URL 114

N

Network Common Data Form (NetCDF) 11
non-interactive backend
  versus interactive backend 7
Not a Number (NaN) 62
NumPy structured array 42

P

PickEvent event 24
picking 38-40
Plot.ly
  URL 114
prettyplotlib
  URL 114
primitives 14-16
pylab_setup() 120

Q

Qt library 135-139, 146, 147

R

radio button 95-98
recipes 69

Thank you for buying
Interactive Applications Using Matplotlib

About Packt Publishing

Packt, pronounced 'packed', published its first book, *Mastering phpMyAdmin for Effective MySQL Management,* in April 2004, and subsequently continued to specialize in publishing highly focused books on specific technologies and solutions.

Our books and publications share the experiences of your fellow IT professionals in adapting and customizing today's systems, applications, and frameworks. Our solution-based books give you the knowledge and power to customize the software and technologies you're using to get the job done. Packt books are more specific and less general than the IT books you have seen in the past. Our unique business model allows us to bring you more focused information, giving you more of what you need to know, and less of what you don't.

Packt is a modern yet unique publishing company that focuses on producing quality, cutting-edge books for communities of developers, administrators, and newbies alike. For more information, please visit our website at www.packtpub.com.

About Packt Open Source

In 2010, Packt launched two new brands, Packt Open Source and Packt Enterprise, in order to continue its focus on specialization. This book is part of the Packt Open Source brand, home to books published on software built around open source licenses, and offering information to anybody from advanced developers to budding web designers. The Open Source brand also runs Packt's Open Source Royalty Scheme, by which Packt gives a royalty to each open source project about whose software a book is sold.

Writing for Packt

We welcome all inquiries from people who are interested in authoring. Book proposals should be sent to author@packtpub.com. If your book idea is still at an early stage and you would like to discuss it first before writing a formal book proposal, then please contact us; one of our commissioning editors will get in touch with you.

We're not just looking for published authors; if you have strong technical skills but no writing experience, our experienced editors can help you develop a writing career, or simply get some additional reward for your expertise.

[PACKT] open source
PUBLISHING
community experience distilled

Matplotlib for Python Developers

Matplotlib for Python Developers

Build remarkable publication-quality plots the easy way

Sandro Tosi

PACKT

Matplotlib for Python Developers

ISBN: 978-1-84719-790-0   Paperback: 308 pages

Build remarkable publication-quality plots the easy way

1. Create high quality 2D plots by using Matplotlib productively.

2. Incremental introduction to Matplotlib, from the ground up to advanced levels.

3. Embed Matplotlib in GTK+, Qt, and wxWidgets applications as well as web sites to utilize them in Python applications.

4. Deploy Matplotlib in web applications and expose it on the Web using popular web frameworks such as Pylons and Django.

matplotlib Plotting Cookbook

Learn how to create professional scientific plots using matplotlib, with more than 60 recipes that cover common use cases

Alexandre Devert

[   ] open source

matplotlib Plotting Cookbook

ISBN: 978-1-84951-326-5   Paperback: 222 pages

Learn how to create professional scientific plots using matplotlib, with more than 60 recipes that cover common use cases

1. Learn plotting with self-contained, practical examples that cover common use cases.

2. Build your own solutions with the orthogonal recipes.

3. Learn to customize and combine basic plots to make sophisticated figures.

Please check **www.PacktPub.com** for information on our titles

Learning IPython for Interactive Computing and Data Visualization

ISBN: 978-1-78216-993-2   Paperback: 138 pages

Learn IPython for interactive Python programming, high-performance numerical computing, and data visualization

1. A practical step-by-step tutorial which will help you to replace the Python console with the powerful IPython command-line interface.

2. Use the IPython notebook to modernize the way you interact with Python.

3. Perform highly efficient computations with NumPy and Pandas.

IPython Notebook Essentials

ISBN: 978-1-78398-834-1   Paperback: 190 pages

Compute scientific data and execute code interactively with NumPy and SciPy

1. Perform Computational Analysis interactively.

2. Create quality displays using matplotlib and Python Data Analysis.

3. Step-by-step guide with a rich set of examples and a thorough presentation of The IPython Notebook.

Made in the USA
Middletown, DE
09 October 2017